UNCERTAINTY

EXPERIMENTS IN MAKING FROM THE CHINESE COUNTRYSIDE

ORO

JOHN LIN
OLIVIER OTTEVAERE

CONTENTS

Introduction 7

Part 1: Uncertainty

1 Innate Material 17
2 Redefining the Collective 67
3 Translating Craft 119
4 Structures of Change 177
5 Responsive Formworks 245

Part 2: Certainty

1 Crest 282
2 Lantern 286
3 Window-Stair 290
4 Stair-Tower 294
5 Wind And Rain Bridge 300
6 Sun Room 304
7 Pinch 310
8 Sweep 314
9 Warp 318
10 Wavelength 326

Right: The working model of the Stair-Tower project used as main communication tool with the carpenters on site.

INTRODUCTION

The tiling pattern of the stone coating of the *sacello* (or small chapel) is one of the most carefully designed elements of Scarpa's Castelvecchio project. This is reflected in a set of drawings that show some areas as clearly and forcefully indicated while others remain vague and ambiguous. At first glance the drawings are seemingly unfinished, yet Scarpa considered every detail. A remarkable story is contained in the handwritten text along the outside margins. Clearly meant as instructions for workers, the notes are directed at specific people, with admonishments, "Rudella, Pay Attention! Damn!" or "Call Parini!" They display frustration, but also a strong sense of familiarity. Existing unknowns and yet to be decided issues are acknowledged in the phrase "to be considered for construction." Some comments display trust in the builders such as "14 multiples + tolerance."

It may be that *tolerance* is what this document best describes—an implicit understanding of the need to collaborate with those who build, resulting in a shared responsibility for resolving problems. The document reveals an obsessive attention to detail, and yet the wall is not drawn explicitly. In this way it is perhaps the exemplar of the working drawing; it goes beyond a set of instructions, but is a transcript of a process, a record of the negotiations between the one who conceives and the one who executes—all the while anticipating the unknown. It reveals a dialogue that is at once intimate, attentive, and contestable. The drawing accepts the limits of design, indicating a clear demarcation between what can and cannot be controlled. Ultimately it is a portrait of a control freak, but in the absolute sense, where the need for exactitude as well as tolerance are both clearly determined. Looking at the final result, the tiling on the *sacello* appears at once random with a barely discernable logic yet contributing to a sense of mysterious order. It has a quality of the spontaneous, so rarely encountered in architecture, and not so easily achieved. Perhaps every architectural project contains a latent story of negotiation and struggle with indeterminacy; attributes typically muted in its final completion, but what if it could be enhanced instead?

Architecture is a profession in which the process of making the final work, or the construction, is almost entirely carried out by others. Due to this situation—a simple fact that distinguishes architecture from many other cultural and artistic productions—architects are self-consciously aware of the difference between design and execution, and by extension the distance separating theory and practice. The making of a work of architecture is often experienced as a struggle to bridge this gap, all the while trying to maintain the initial vision. This book tells a different story, about how things actually come to be built; within it are stories of design, not as preconceived ideas, but often as a process of trial and error resulting from a dialogue between designers and builders, students and villagers. The book traces a back-and-forth journey and transmission of ideas between studios and labs at the University of Hong Kong and project sites throughout rural China. Rather than testimonials of the conquest of uncertainty, these projects embrace it.

Presented in this book are examples taken from a series of design and build experiments conducted by the Department of Architecture at the University of Hong Kong over the past ten years. Looking back on these projects, we began to ask ourselves where do our designs come from? A common presumption is that design precedes implementation, with the former occurring in a laboratory while the latter occurs in the field; a contrast between a controlled setting, for conceiving ideas, with an unpredictable site for intervening in. In our work, we have found that these two scenarios are not independent, but mutually influence each other; where stages of brainstorming, prototyping, design development, and implementation becoming blurred and on occasion, interchangeable. In making our work, we often travel between the university in Hong Kong and sites in China, which couldn't be more contrasting, even if they are in relative close proximity. One question keeps re-occurring: how can we harness the technological, economic, social, and political differences between the city and the countryside?

The ambiguity that exists between sites of design and construction is demonstrated in Donn Holohan's Sun Room, where a crucial physical device at the top of the pavilion (responsible for regulating the overall structural geometry) required a level of precise construction that could only be prototyped and shipped from our university in Hong Kong, while the bamboo surface itself could not be "designed" in advance (impossible to draw or describe accurately) but had to be resolved entirely in-situ through the expertise of traditional bamboo weavers. Between the structure of the pavilion and its surface, two very different understandings of what it means to be precise are demonstrated: either requiring more accuracy or greater approximation. The book contains many examples of creative processes that necessitate re-inventing the tools of design, often as a consequence of bringing together digital, robotic, and traditional methods of building.

To think carefully about how to communicate became a common and surprising source of inspiration in all our projects. As foreign-born architects trained abroad (in addition to the challenge of working in remote sites with highly specific local Chinese dialects) cultural differences were an ever-present difficulty. The lack of a common spoken language placed emphasis on drawing as the principle means of "conversation about design." The usual role of the drawing in making architecture has an explicit and implicit function: to describe the building so that it can be built by others—the aim to predict, anticipate, and control the process of construction. Our experiments with drawing as illustrated throughout this book, demonstrate the ways in which drawing allowed us to overcome unknowns; whether related to the material, the site, or even unstable political and economic conditions. Could the drawing "open up" the project to unexpected forces, and in turn allow a quality of the spontaneous to enter and embed itself into the work? We've discovered that communication and miscommunication can both lead to a wellspring of ideas.

Pinch, Sweep, and Warp was the beginning of an ongoing collaboration with a newly established wood contractor. Ironically, the houses he was building were entirely based on western notions of timber-frame construction, as opposed to the rich culture of wooden houses building in China. We quickly realized that many of our initial drawings were ignored or proved unnecessary. Faced with multiple unknowns (as in Pinch, where the foundation wall was built independently by the local government); it pushed us to develop a system of relational measurement principles—a method inspired by Chinese traditional timber craft, where accuracy is the result of assimilated tolerances not exact calculation. In these projects, we had to find ways of compensating for the disengagement between the roof above and a ground condition that could not be surveyed or known beforehand. Working with standard timber sections, we developed a custom drawing language: a strategic set of principles anchored in simple linear geometries while enabling us to construct complex and responsive structures. The system allowed for the roof and ground to be independently changing entities while the trusses adapted to varying profiles.

The more time we spent working with experienced self-builders with their own craft tradition, it made sense to not adhere to any established drawing standards. Looking back, we realize the ability to implement projects relied less on detailed instruction, but adaptability and the intuition of our "untrained" builders. This created a space of tolerance by balancing the skills and know-how of the professional builder alongside the self-builder. In Bernard Rudofsky's introduction to the 1964 exhibition *Architecture Without Architects* at the Museum of Modern Art, New York, he describes these builders variously as "spontaneous" and refers to their "untutored imagination." Although by the standards of modern construction, spontaneity is not usually a good thing; we have often witnessed how it was exactly this trait in our builders, unaccustomed to deferring their inherent ingenuity in favor of formulaic approaches, that solved the most difficult and unexpected problems.

In the *tulou* (large earthen-walled collective houses in southern China) renovation projects, Stair-Tower and Window-Stair, the potential of local craftspeople was unleashed when we paired them with the timber contractors from Pinch, Sweep, and Warp. Together in this working hybrid, the task to repair and renovate the ancient structures became an experiment in collective design and decision making. Contributions to the final outcome were made by students, villagers, contractors, and local craftspeople alike. Due to the complexity of the project, situated within a 300-year-old historical and highly detailed vernacular building, our approach had to consider each design element, structure, sitting platforms, circulation, façade, etc., as a set of principle rules that could be easily and independently adapted by builders. By breaking down the role of the designer and builder and, for that matter the role of teacher, researcher, and practitioner, this project is an expression of collective design.

Wavelengths is the final project presented in this book because it brings previous threads of investigation together. The story of this project can be traced to early design studios with students, experimenting with different casting techniques including with fabric over bamboo formwork. The convergence of pure laboratory explorations and the geometrical strategies of Pinch, Sweep, and Warp resulted in a hybrid wood and concrete structure imbued with a sense of the naturesque. Wavelengths is a culmination of approaches derived through various investigations. The entire collection of work can be viewed as independent ideas with the potential to create recombinant and expanding possibilities for further work.

Working closely with skilled builders from a very different culture of making has altered our notions about control; challenging the contemporary architect's paradigm of design and construction based around the assertion of control. Perhaps the role of the architect can be reconsidered within an alternative matrix of simultaneous and spontaneous problem solving. As a whole, the book reveals a space for design that is no longer linear; a space that is complex, collaborative, contradictory, and messy but ultimately highly tolerant. We've been deeply affected by the collective nature of building with rural communities—as our own collaborative mixtures over these dozen projects attests.

As the result of a design process that traversed the boundaries between urban Hong Kong and rural China, each project is imprinted with geopolitical realities. These remarkable and diffuse explorations can be attributed to the differences in their contextual situations. Some were urgent post-earthquake reconstructions, often adapting to extreme topographies or taking place in the midst of major urbanizing transformations, whereas other experiments occurred in forgotten villages with left-behind craftspeople and their disappearing building cultures. Looking back, we realized that the variety manifested in this collection of projects is a direct reflection of the incredible diversity of climates, locations, and conditions that underlie the ongoing Chinese urbanization experiment. The focus here is not on the *what* but the *how*, as each project engages with its own set of limiting factors or unideal situations. They are stories of design, overcoming, and even embracing adverse situations in order to discover some hidden advantage. Each chapter explores a new attempt to revert seemingly challenging limitations (particularly those which the architect cannot exert control over) and turn these into novel building approaches.

This book is a reflection on our work, not only through text and images, but crucially, through the process of making drawings; as a means of design and a means of building, where drawings represent ways of control and inversely perhaps, what should not be controlled. This is not new, as the issue of control is endemic to the process of making architecture. However, learning to embrace it is one of the major lessons we've learned in over ten years of project making in the Chinese countryside. It has allowed us to look back and realize a fundamental truth: the projects described here could not have happened anywhere else, because of how they adapt to the specific logistical, financial, political, and social challenges found in China today. Looking back on the Chinese urbanization experiment begun over forty years ago, one is reminded of an aphorism by Deng Xiaoping, who was at the start of it all: "to cross the river by feeling the stones." As we continue to explore and work in this context, we find ourselves doing the same thing.

PART 1
UNCERTAINTY

INNATE MATERIAL

This is how we typically build. We build with materials, with the help of drawn instructions, and a pre-defined work process, to assemble an architectural product that we expect to have a certain permanence and soundness. These are the standard and expected conditions by which architecture is generally made. Yet, when it comes to bamboo construction, these four presumptions are radically challenged in the way that each of these aspects—material, drawing, working process and permanency—can both inform and challenge one another to potentially reroute the design process in unexpected ways and redefine a building hierarchy that defies the norm.

Contextually, there is much to learn about the way bamboo is used in Hong Kong. The city remains one of the last urban centers globally to maintain its longstanding tradition of building with the plant. It is still used today in temporary structures such as scaffoldings for erecting skyscrapers or seasonally assembled and disassembled Cantonese opera theaters, demonstrating both the expediency and versatility of working directly in-situ with this original construction material. However, the seemingly ad hoc and informal nature of bamboo construction belies the skill and knowhow required to assemble it.

Material

Unlike steel or even timber—which are more standard and industrial, yet also more consuming and demanding to work with—bamboo harvests the very best of a natural, cheap, fast-growing, sustainable, and highly available material. If considered as an individual pole, yes, it is irregular in section, crooked in length, and can bend or fatigue easily over time

Right: Earth work and landscaping of the Crest project after construction

by nature of being organic and fibrous. Yet, when addressed as an assembly of linear elements, its construction system is made relatively effortless, not just by being a light material easy to handle, but mainly in the way poles are quickly and flexibly hand tied together. This tying technique largely bypasses the material's irregularities or inconsistency, which is a challenging hurdle in conventional joinery. It also eliminates any need for tolerances that these structural assemblies would otherwise require if, for example, joined mechanically. Instead, this technique engenders more freedom and diversity in the range and types of structures that can be conceived.

Set of instructions

What is most impressive about these impromptu bamboo structures is that they are made without the need of any drawings. It is rare for any types of construction nowadays not to be prescribed by a set of graphic instructions that ensure the outcome is more controllable and predictable. The absence of instructional drawings with this particular material portrays a process of building that is rather informal: intuitive but also relatively high-risk. This is especially true when considering complications of liability in today's building industry, where all constructional aspects and logistics are registered in the working documents as trace of accountability.

Instead, in Hong Kong, all bamboo constructional decisions are directly taken on site by the craftspeople, without reliance on structural calculations or specifications, and entirely flexible and reactionary to the conditions in front of them. Design and constructional decisions have become one; they are relational and based on how big a project needs to be in relation to the obtainable sizes—length and diameter—of bamboo poles. At last, conventionally scaled drawings have made way for a new metric: the bamboo pole itself, utilized essentially as a measuring stick in-situ. This suggests a different way of thinking, design decisions can be informed by this direct approach to prototyping with the material itself and, by extension, with its specific properties. Could a structure be potentially rendered further expressive through the manipulation or rather amplification of its material forces, such as tension and compression?

Working process

Bamboo craftspeople are not just regular construction workers, but artisans. They are part of a skilled trade, rooted in tradition passed down through generations, which takes time and physical effort to master. The tradition in Hong Kong has become endangered due to the intense physical labor it demands, with the work mainly carried out in extreme weather conditions of rain, heat, and humidity for too little compensation given the expertise required.

However, this inherited specialty can also create a culture of building that is rather stubborn or less accessible than other trades, as bamboo craftspeople are more reticent to deviate from their known techniques. Namely, the specific knowledge these skilled workers have accumulated over time makes it more difficult for them to be receptive to other methods of building with bamboo, or to be amenable to alternative modes of assembly (e.g., prefabricated components). This constraint is at times frustrating, particularly if one wants to actively participate in the process of construction of new kinds of projects.

Which other forms of collaboration between designers and local builders would need to take place in order to negotiate this divide between traditional craft and more contemporary design outputs made in bamboo? In which ways would the design approach have to evolve to be able to adapt to existing working methods? Could an iterative process between design and prototyping with the material serve to create a feedback loop between the adaptation and integration of one expertise over the other—between design and making?

It is true that the construction procedure that bamboo workers generally adopt is additive, yet it is mostly non-hierarchical, especially in putting up scaffoldings. Unlike in architecture projects, distinctive archetypes such as column, beam, wall, and roof are not recognized parts of the essential building order in bamboo structures. Rather, the act of building is linear, and culminates in impressive edifices made of countless bamboo poles, manually tied together, assembled in situ one stick at the time.

The part-to-whole relationship in these types of constructions is relatively blurred or non-discrete, since the parts are dominant. Here, they are less recognizable as single entities and as a result allow room for a more fluid and uninterrupted reading of the whole. In embracing this unique property, could a hierarchical assembly—more related to archetypes pertinent to architecture—be implemented with bamboo while maintaining the continuous and growing reading of the whole as manifested by these informal constructions? If so, how could this be achieved via different constructional methods while still being able to be realized by teams of local builders?

A seasoned bamboo construction worker is often recognized by the mastery of his knots gained over time. The way knots bundle and splice bamboo poles together—in order to reach greater heights and larger building sizes—involves not only specialized know-how but also measured intuitions at the construction site. The straight intricacy of tying an unrestricted number of circular poles together, coming from and going in any possible directions, gives the structural system a great deal of flexibility in what can be made three-dimensionally and in the form in which a structure can grow. What the ties offer is the possibility of a building system without static joints or breaks (e.g., poles mainly butting or arrested against each other). Instead, joints are eschewed altogether, allowing for a continuous and expanding assembly of poles with no identifiable separate parts. Could one sustain this reading of growth and fluidity with contemporary structures by means of alternative types of joints? Could compound joints, for example, still provide smooth transitions between a bundle of connecting elements and convey a non-static reading of space?

Temporary versus permanent

Seasonal Cantonese theaters in Hong Kong are more hierarchical or nuanced than scaffoldings, and also more complex to build in comparison. It usually takes a team of six to nine workers about two weeks to complete such provisional edifice. The size of the theater, both in plan and in section, is often defined proportionally by how big the stage needs to be. Construction begins with erecting four straight and flat vertical lattices demarcating the envelope on the perimeter, followed by a pitched roof called the "sky cover." Poles are crossed, spliced, and all tied together. For the most part, they are outsourced from China in lengths of more or less 20ft. Lastly, the structure is entirely covered with thin zinc sheets providing shading and waterproofing. Once the season is over, theaters are then disassembled pole by pole and their materials completely recycled.

The difference between temporary versus permanent is critical in the way the design of a building is conceived. Somehow, by virtue of being temporary, these types of bamboo structures hold the possibility to re-interpret and experiment with what can be done with a specific material on site in a way that permanent edifices don't allow. Because of their lasting imperatives, permanent structures tend to rely more on existing, tested, and accepted knowledge and are less receptive to experimentation or hypothetical construction. Could this very direct and expeditious way of working with bamboo open up new trajectories in rethinking the role and impact of design vis-à-vis building? If so, how would typical practices need to change and adapt in order to exploit new architectural potentials drawn from engaging with the material hands-on at the construction site with as little drawing instructions as necessary?

Bamboo theaters are actually hybrid buildings made of fir beams for the main structural elements, like columns, ledgers, and rafters. Fir beams (referred here as "masts") are used in this instance in favor of bamboo poles (the "needles") because they are less susceptible to bending over time or to flex under loading. After being secured in their respective positions, they are complemented by numerous bamboo poles, spanning in different directions. In making up the majority of the structure, bamboo act as immediate bracings to stabilize the entire structure. In this case, columns, beams, walls, and roof demarcate a first order between recognizable elements. Yet, by being further blurred with the addition of countless (bamboo) reinforcements, the material interior of the theater presents itself as a unified physical space, even though devised of a disguised or semi-hierarchal assembly. How could this unique characteristic be sustained when addressing a lasting structural hierarchy? What alternative design procedure needs to arise in order for an intuitive structure to emerge, informed through a series of material and constructional feedbacks laid out by local craftsmen?

Crest and Lantern

These two buildings are two experiments made in bamboo, whose design-build experience strives to address some of the questions raised above. Both constructions were conducted via teaching at the University of Hong Kong and built with architecture students in remote sites in China (Anji County, Zhejiang Province). They are the results of two national university building competitions held every two years during the course of the summer. For each project, the brief was to demonstrate how bamboo as an ancient material could be inventively reconsidered beyond its vernacular connotations in the making of contemporary architecture, while still being able to be constructed with the support of local craftspeople.

Material

In Crest, bamboo was tested via a family of compound joints, similar in type, but of all different geometries and sizes to support an irregular roof. Rising from a concrete plinth, a field of columns fan out in opposite directions to delineate a series of rooflines of constantly changing depths. In order to transfer the structure uninterrupted from column to roof, unique joints had to be devised; joints made of numerous bamboo poles that set out to blur any preestablished hierarchy between the architectural elements. To achieve this, multiple joints were introduced within one column assembly in order to maintain a continuous spatial reading of the entire structure: some where bamboo poles had to bypass each other to provide continuity, others where poles had to stop by butting against one another to make way for more primary elements. This established a necessary hierarchy between singular poles within the joints themselves, as a means to erase the divisions between distinct archetypes (e.g., column to beam to roof). As a result, the joints provided smoother transitions from vertical props (columns) to horizontal space-frame (roof). The experiment tested how robustly this joining technique would perform across the entire irregular structure in challenging and further redefining its part-to-whole relationship. In return, a unique taxonomy of varied three-dimensional joints emerged, serving as the main conceptual driver and generator of the project.

In the case of Lantern, bamboo as material was further experimented with by directly acting on its unique fibrous property. Through the use of a known local technique—heat and steam bending—the flexing of elements was actively encouraged to assess the capacity of tensile forces to amplify the structural reading and spatial experiences of the project. Could active force, in and of itself, be the catalyst from which bamboo architecture gets further improved in ways that other kinds of materials can't enable? And if so, what should the design process include to allow for such material behaviors to become complicit to the ultimate structural performance of the project? In hindsight, what would the constrains and benefits of such an immediate design approach be?

In general, the development of Lantern evolved from Crest not only in how some of the learnt joining techniques were refined, but mostly in the way that material properties were further utilized in a more intuitive and innate manner. The bending of some of the elements not only entirely unified the reading of the structure, but also made the viewer conscious of the tensile forces exerted on the material itself.

Set of Instructions

The governing geometries for both projects were first rationalized into a sequence of two-dimensional bays, each evolving from column to truss. The changing bays were organized transversally for Crest and radially for Lantern. Drawings of each bay instructed the local workers of the exact geometrical position of its respective roofline. The height of the top ridges needed to be carefully controlled in order to ensure the proper holistic fitting of the overall structure, but the remaining geometry of each bay accounted for a larger degree of tolerance to absorb any material uncertainty and some of the unpredictability coming with onsite craftsmanship. Once built they served as templates, guiding the rest of the in-situ construction that spanned in the other directions until completed. As for the final material composition of each bay—layering and joining of poles—a process of back and forth exchanges through mockups and sketches between the design team and local builders established the guiding principles of their constructional hierarchy based on the locally available species. In other words, design here was highly influenced or cyclically informed not only by how something was going to be built in a practical manner, but also through negotiating local expertise and resources while keeping in step with the projected architectural ambitions of the projects. Minimal building instructions were delivered not just through drawings but more significantly through physical models that matured over the course of back and forth conversations with the local contractor throughout the design process.

In the end, both structures were not predetermined, calculated, nor verified by engineers. Instead, they were arrived at intuitively and progressively through an empirical process between the act of prototyping and its design responses. In reflection, the direct feedback given from working with the material and its active properties incrementally allowed for a closer understanding and approximation of the structure's natural behavior and physical performance.

Working Process

Both projects began with site visits and studies with no preconceived design in mind. Ultimately, it was key that the essence of their spatial, structural, and material organizations would become site responsive and not stand-alone or imported objects. To reinforce this sense of belonging with their natural surroundings, earthworks in the vein of concrete foundations, retaining walls, and slabs embedded within the terrain were designed and first constructed by local builders. What these new ground articulations did was to demarcate a first scalar reference for the intrinsic anchoring of the bamboo structures to come.

The working relationship between students and craftspeople in the construction of the projects was challenging. Although the design of the projects evolved and matured alongside feedback on the construction details, and vice versa, the level of craft required to work with the material made it prohibitively inaccessible to students. Instead, their inputs onsite became one of advising and consulting on the proper execution of the projects' designs and regulatory geometries.

In Crest, ideas of prefabricated components (e.g., a series of branching columns) were contemplated at first to increase quality control, ease assembly, and speed construction time. Yet this was quickly abandoned as it did not fit the manner in which bamboo craftspeople build locally. Their approach to construction was more tailor-made, rendering the process quite time consuming and cumbersome. Eventually, the structure was completely erected one stick at the time, requiring each of the many poles to be independently measured in place, cut, and adjusted until it could be properly fitted in its specific location. Once again, the bamboo pole itself took over the predominance of drawn instructions to become the main analog metric of the project.

The working process in Lantern was relatively similar with the exception that it incorporated a more expedient way to keep control of the global geometry of the structure. The guiding geometry for the project ascends from circle to square to ellipse. At the base, a circular concrete foundation ensured the proper placements of the bamboo columns, evolving into trusses up above to receive a levelled cantilevered steel frame, to then culminate around an elliptical steel ring at the top. These three full-scale figures or lost templates served as live relational devices onsite to guarantee, at three different intervals, an accurate and unified integration of all parts.

Temporary Versus Permanent

Both projects were constructed and their materials treated to last 20 years. Despite their factual permanency, it is the open-endedness and asymmetry of their bamboo structures that give them a sense of temporariness and even temporality. The way the spaces of the projects portray a certain degree of porosity or physical looseness establishes a strong dialogue with their contexts, more precisely with their proximate grounds, as well as intimate visual ties with their surrounding and extensive landscapes.

In Lantern, the openings between the columns at the base vary in sizes. As they scan the surrounding landscape in a 360-degrees panorama, the voids between them progressively contract in some areas and expand in others. Almost curtain-like, this unbalanced circular enfilade of columns presents the occupant with a sense of permeability that is as much active as it is ever-changing. In fact, the constantly fleeting spatial experience between inside and outside discloses an unusual perception of ephemerality; even perhaps a new form of embodied temporariness. This is further exacerbated by the oculus at the top, essentially operating as sundial. The way sunlight penetrates the interior and washes its surfaces is different each day, extending this notion of fugitive space and temporality over its permanent status.

Similarly, in Crest, the collapse of structure is at play—not a literal but a spatial one. Taking advantage of its crescent shape in plan, the project slims out from its deepest structural bay at the middle to mere silhouettes at both ends. At that moment, the visitor is left unwittingly outside as the bamboo structure subsides into two-dimensional profiles, echoing the mountainous landscape beyond. Could this design intent underscore another form of temporariness?

At last, both projects demarcate a material (de)gradation; from solid to lightweight. Firmly grounded in the soil by concrete, their lighter bamboo structures incrementally rise from fields of discrete columns into unified yet irregular filigree space frames, ultimately arresting thin layers of roofs, like tensile membranes. On reflection, this contrast in kinds of materiality—concrete, bamboo, and fabric—and the types of tolerances accounted for between them, offers another reading of temporariness to the experiences of the projects.

EXAMPLE 1: CREST

1. The tensile membrane comes last—must be tailor-made to stretch like a skin on the bamboo structure;

2. Concrete foundation comes first—it will include pedestrian path (check slope!);

3. ! Important ! Longitudinal rooflines govern. If we don't get it right, roof won't fit;

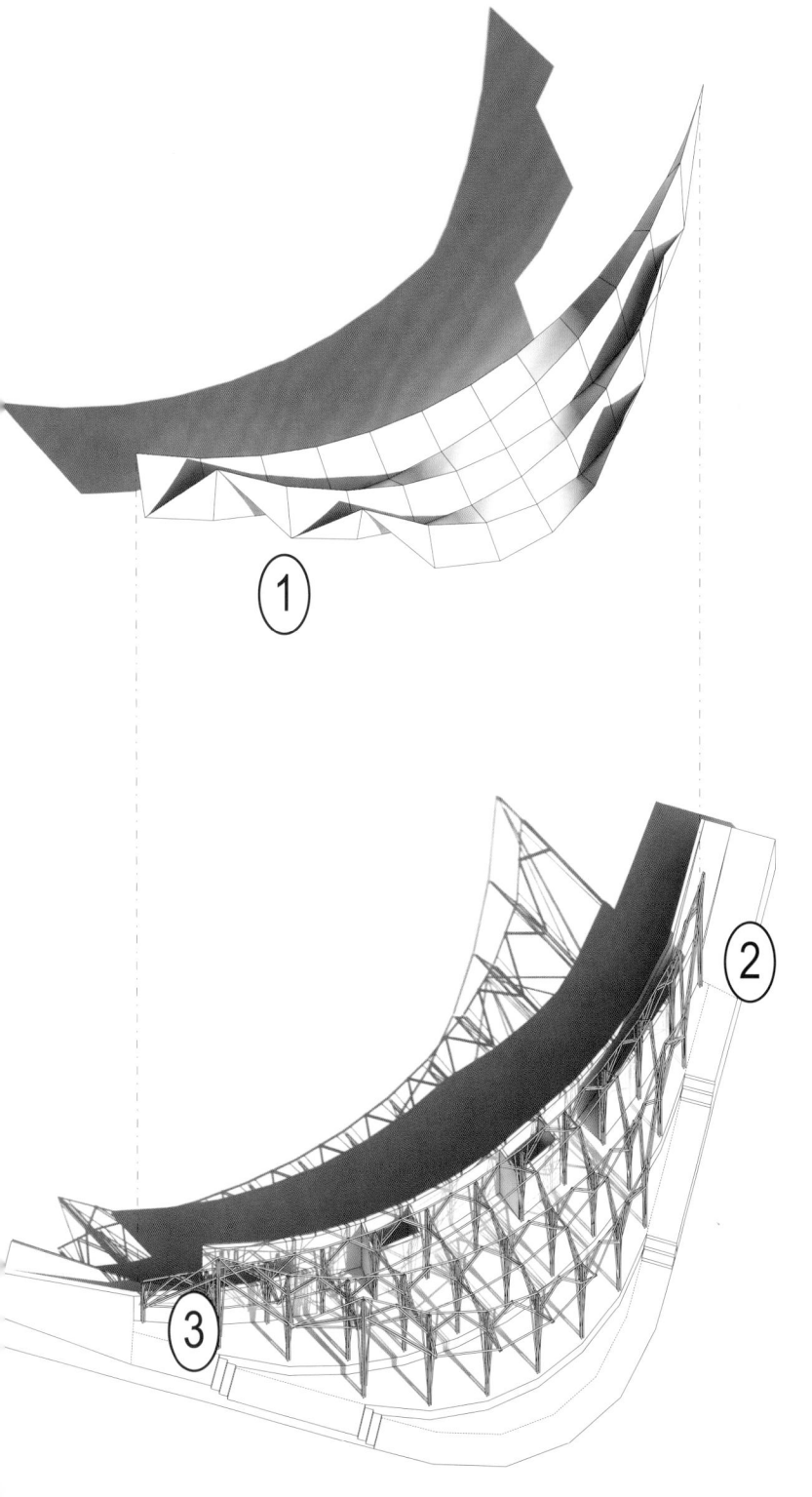

1 The main space will be accessed from this ramp—again, slope to be double checked;

2 Ask contractor about plumbing and electrical systems (kitchen, toilets go against retaining wall);

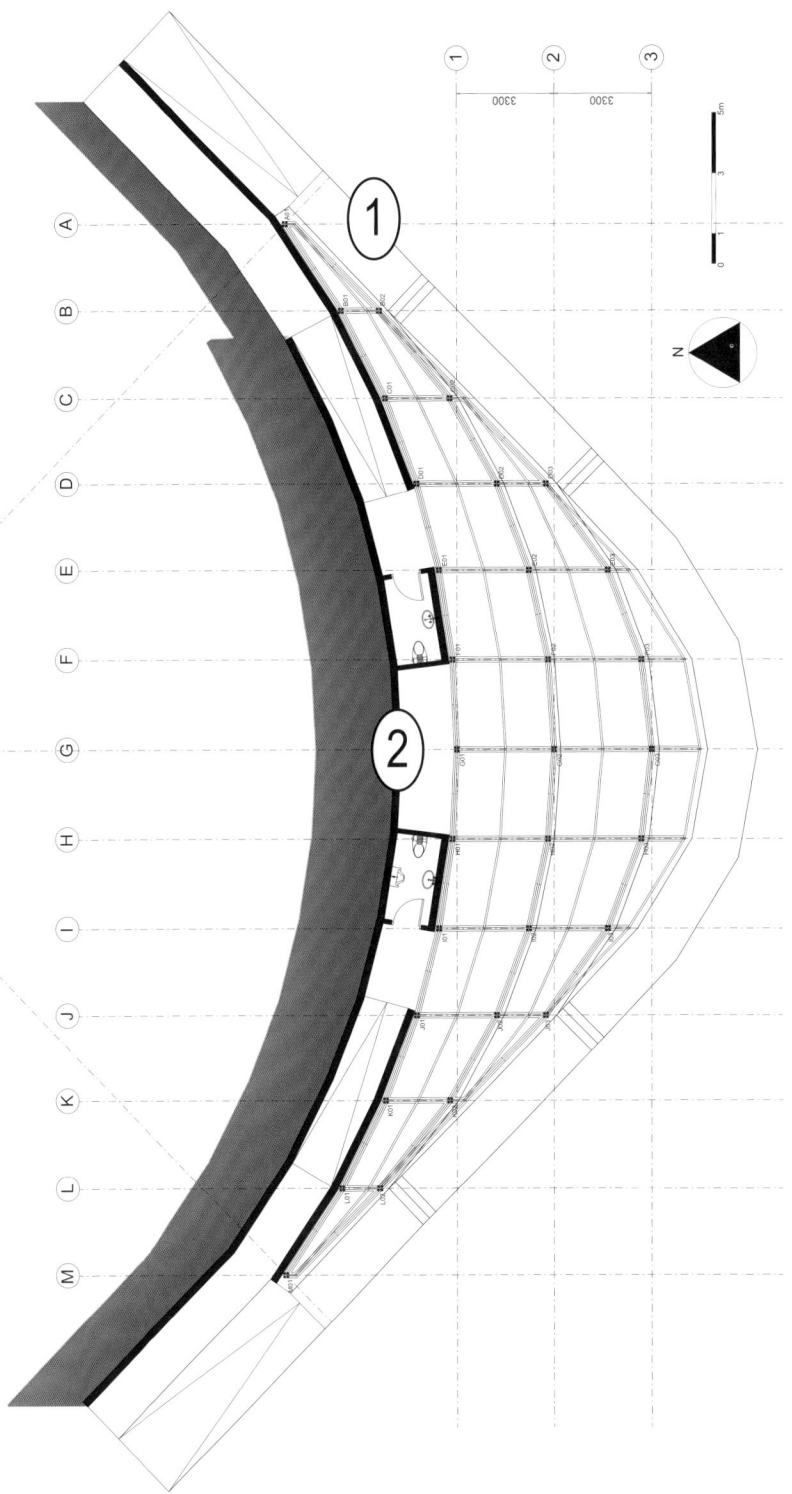

1. Services and secondary ramps sandwiched in between a double retaining wall;

2. Columns' footings must align along the edges of the foundation. It's going to be stepped so we need to find a way to mark them accurately;

3. Make sure contractor understands the sectional lines for the concrete foundation—this plan is for reference—he should have a look at sectional drawings;

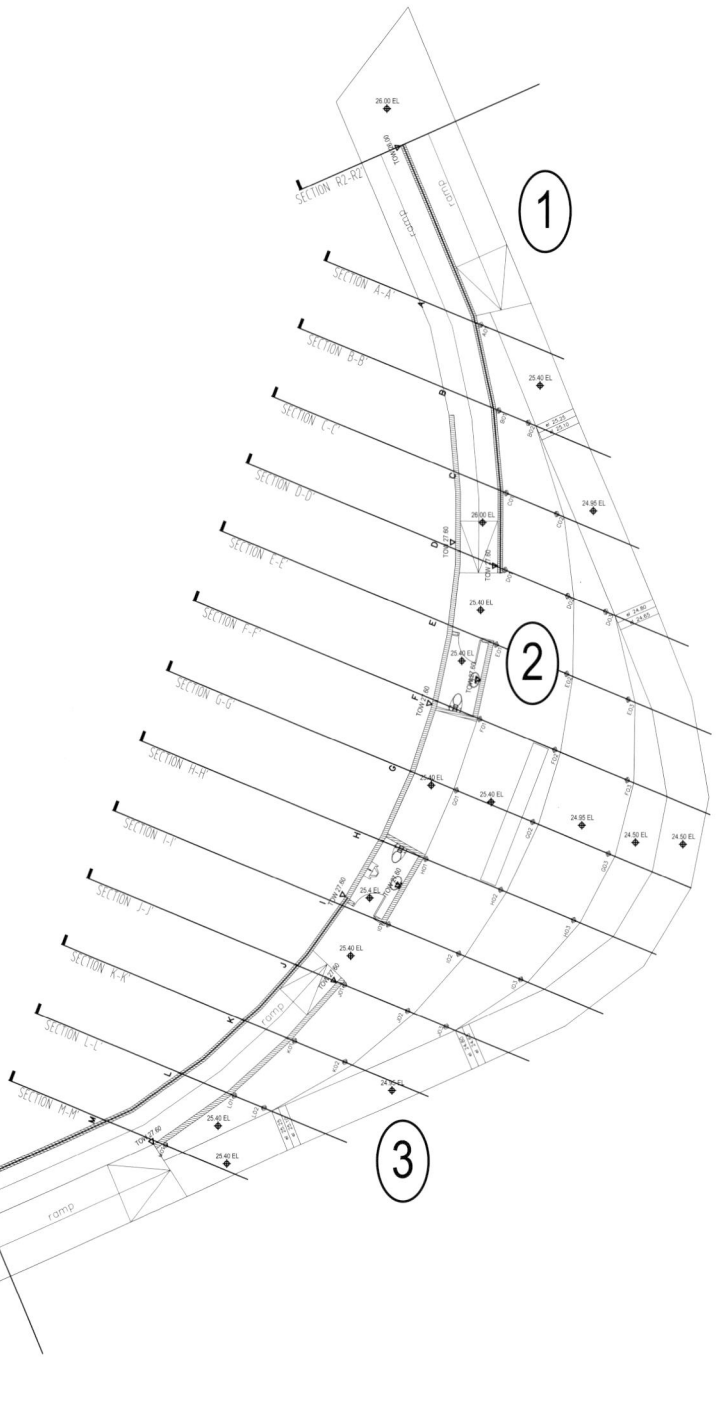

1. FF', GG', HH' cross-sections of expanding and contracting foundation to be checked by contractor!

2. Landscape needs further consideration: how do we integrate the retaining wall into it?

3. Use metal plate for bamboo columns—it should feel they sit effortlessly on the stepped terraces;

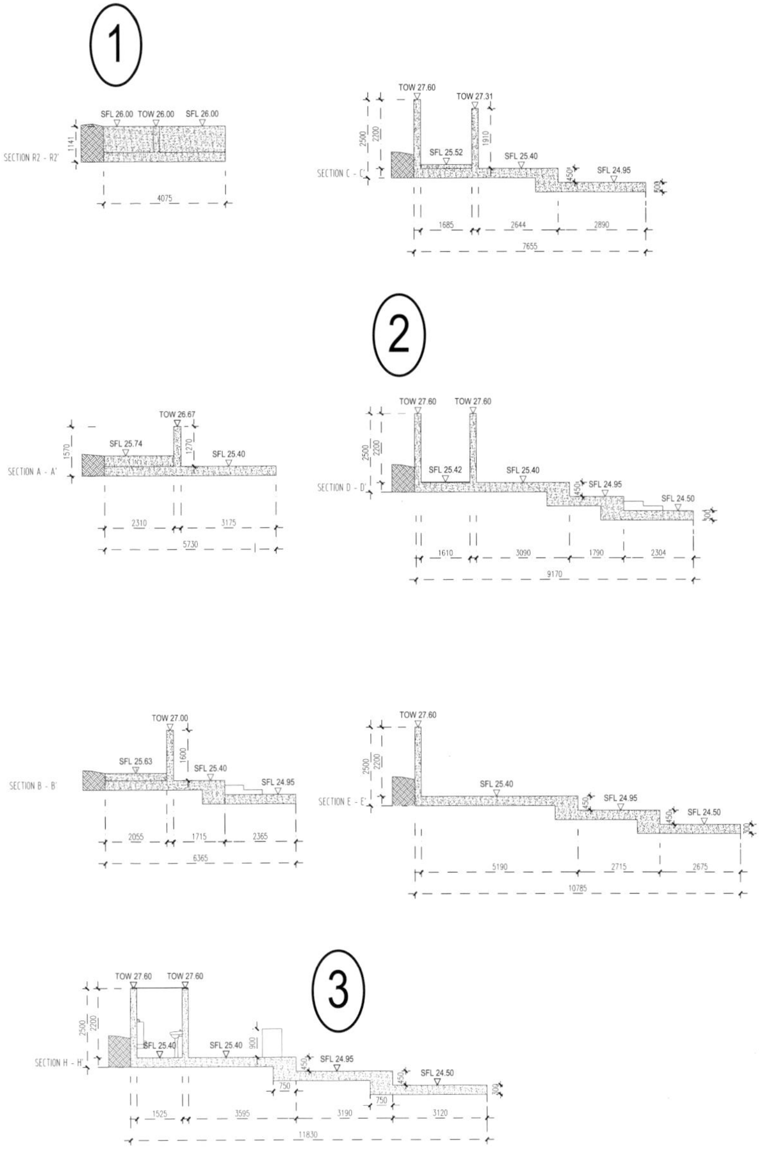

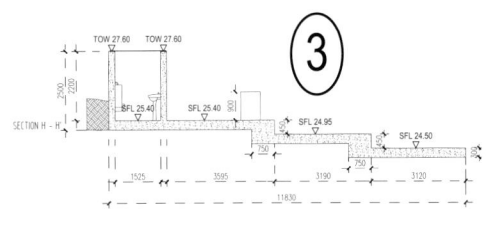

SECTION
SCALE 1:100

1. Bamboo column A01—see reference in plan (section AA')—only one column along the line;

2. Columns at the base fanning out to roofline. See bamboo pole A01-T 940;

3. Roofline. Reference: A01-C 2125; A01-RP 1000
It's extremely important to control it accurately during construction! All rooflines in all drawings should be marked in red—if not, get someone to do it;

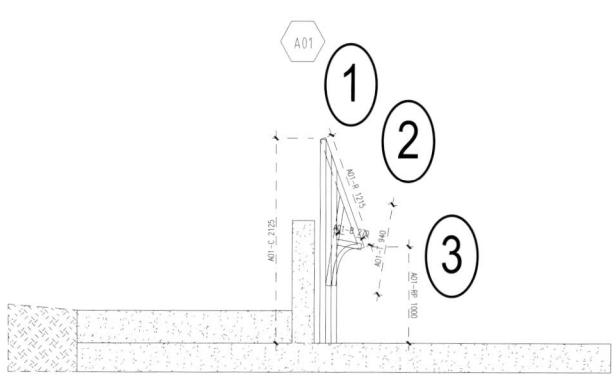
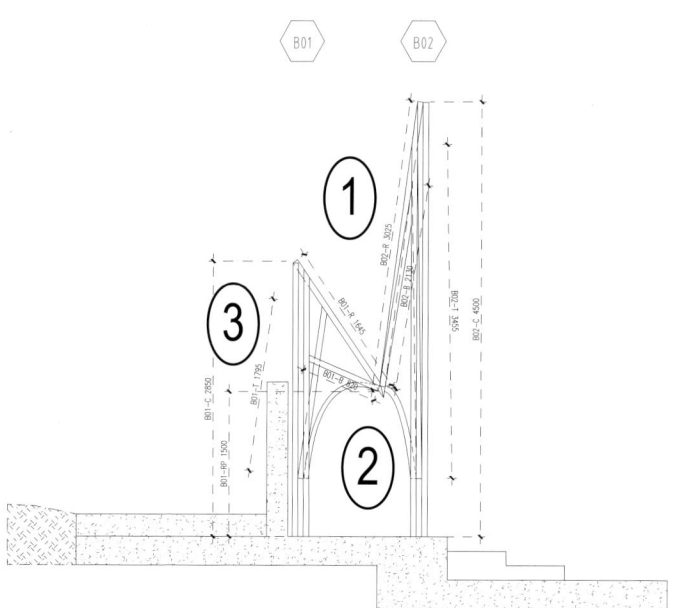

1. Bamboo column A01—see reference in plan (section AA')—only one column along the line;

2. Columns at the base fanning out to roofline. See bamboo pole A01-T 940;

3. Roofline. Reference: A01-C 2125; A01-RP 1000
It's extremely important to control it accurately during construction! All rooflines in all drawings should be marked in red—if not, get someone to do it;

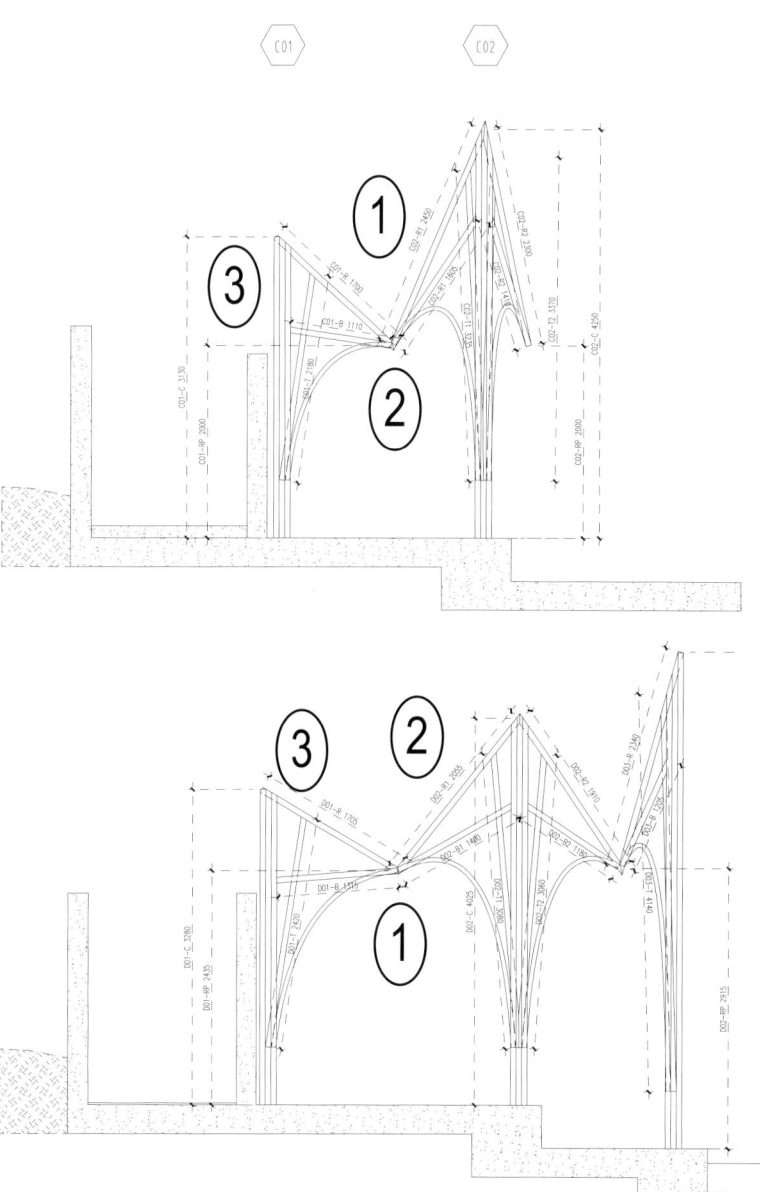

1. Longitudinal bays including all 01 columns (see plan: from A01 to M01);

2. Roof trusses are made of singles layers;

3. Columns are bundles of four bamboo poles;

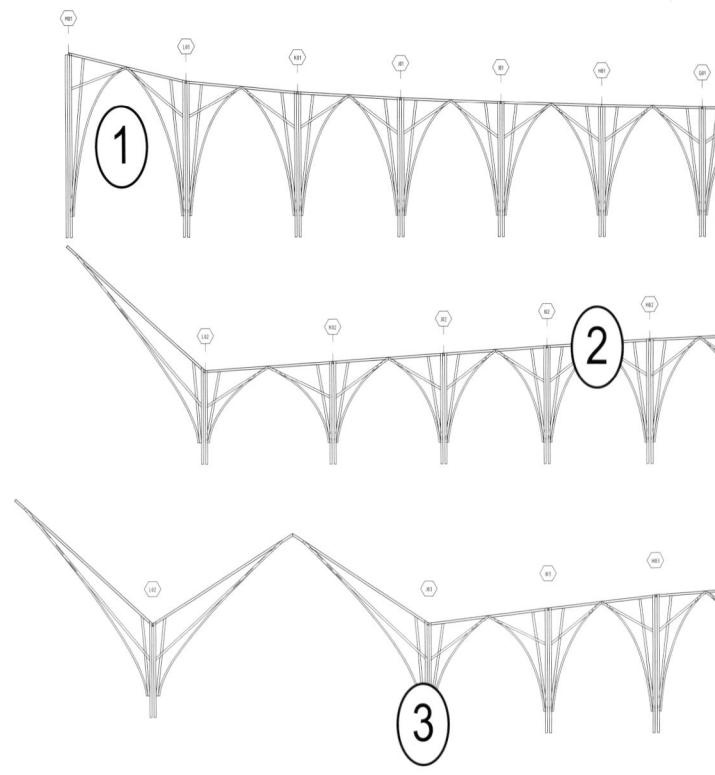

4   Longitudinal bays including all 02 columns (see plan: from B02 to L02—"trusses" A and M only have one column);

5   Longitudinal bays including all 03 columns (see plan: from B02 to L02);

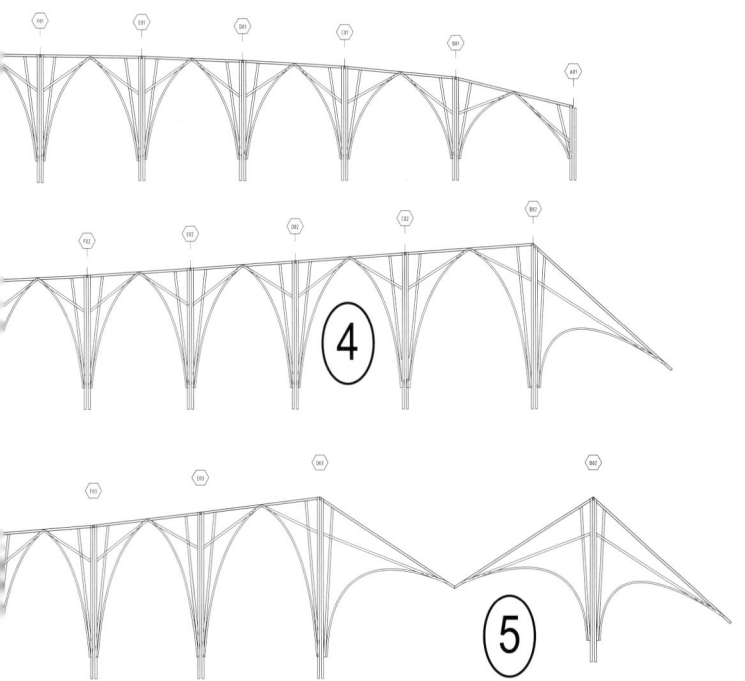

Adjustment onsite of column joints.

Hand-made elliptical cuts for close-fitting assembly.

Columns are the first elements to be erected on top of concrete foundation, transversal trusses come second and longitudinal bays are made last.

EXAMPLE 2: LANTERN

1   Setting out—determine origin point. Construct the X and Y axes on site (Cardinal directions) draw oculus in the southeast quadrant (R1215) tangent to both axes and construct perimeter edge;

2   Segment both as shown clockwise. Construct tangent axis and intersect with R4425 circle from origin to locate column centers;

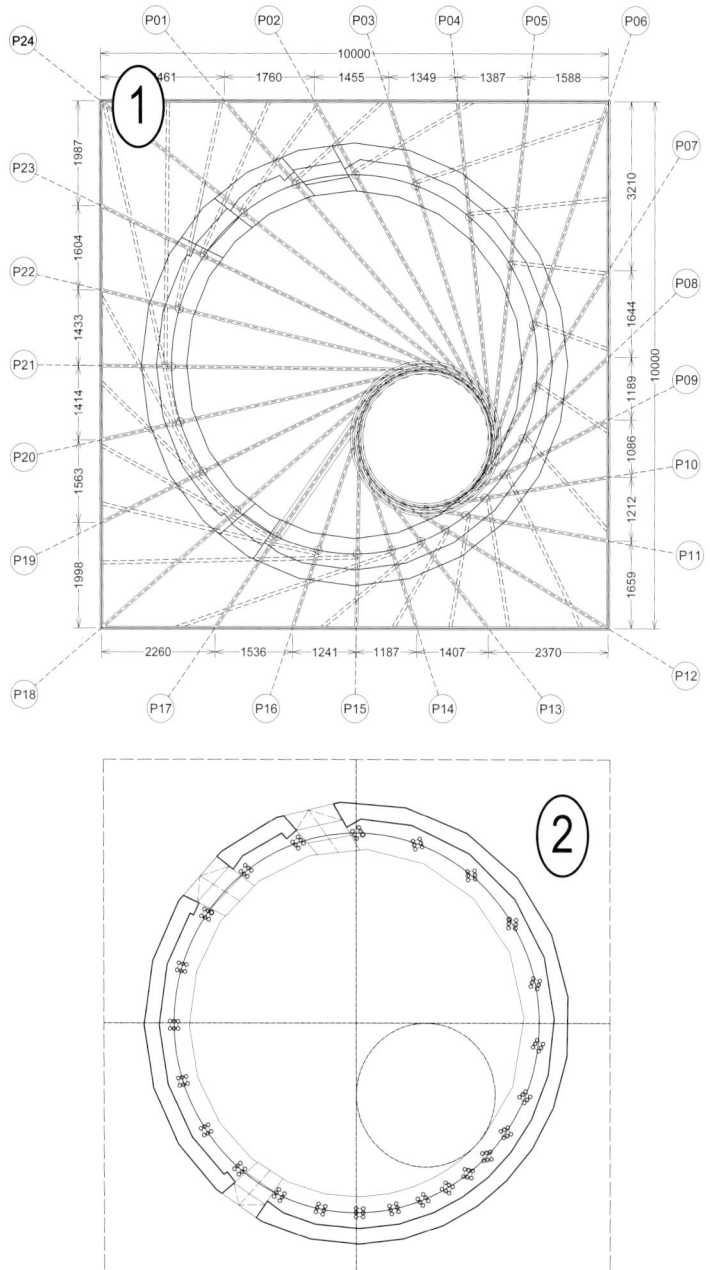

1   Individual trusses are composed of three layers and there are no duplicates. The trusses transform as they revolve tangentially around the oculus;

2   Counter bracing to be applied following the completion of primary structure. Stabilize the edge first using the steel ring beam/gutter before linking the trusses. Important prop and adjust overall level at four corners only remove once entire structure is braced;

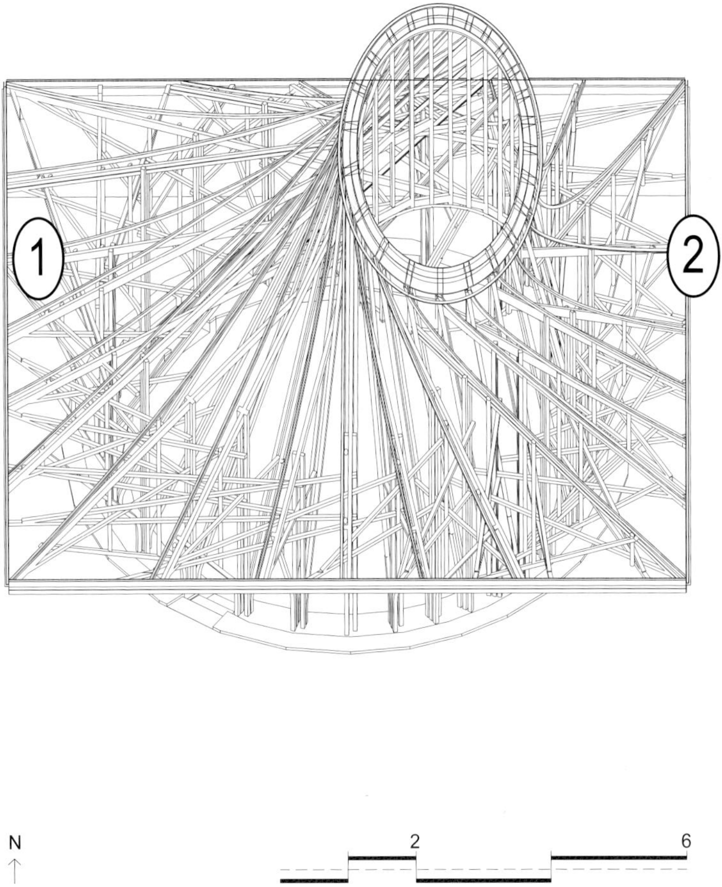

① ②

N
↑

1. Foundations do not match set out! Designed entrances are unworkable must be filled in;

2. Engineers report returned—water table on island is high, reduce depth of foundations by one step no other changes to set out;

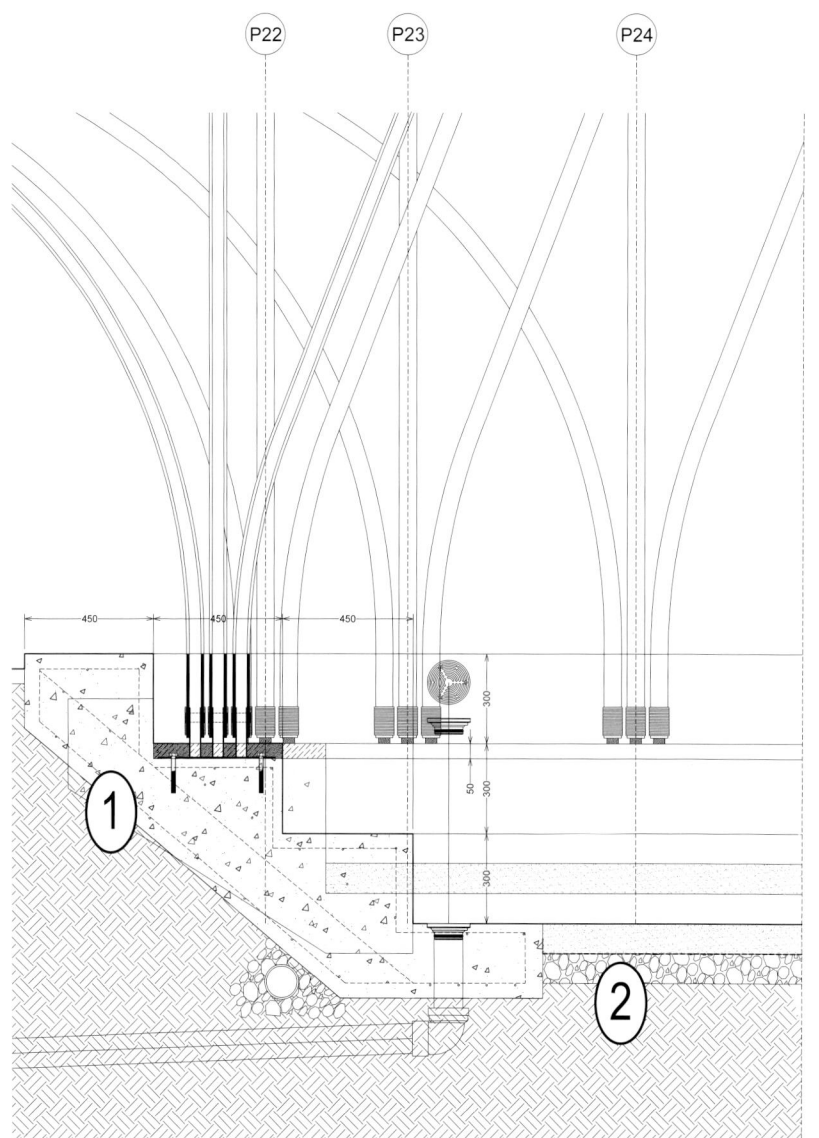

1   No bridge exists to island only site access via small floating pathway—prefabrication of large building element not possible, all work will be in situ;

2   Abandon incremental construction strategy, instead construct individual trusses on ground and "tilt up." This is better use of resources—students can mark and drill locations for joint while craftspeople can cut and assemble —both can help to stand trusses on their steel feet —brace together temporarily until guide ring and steel edge are delivered by fabricator;

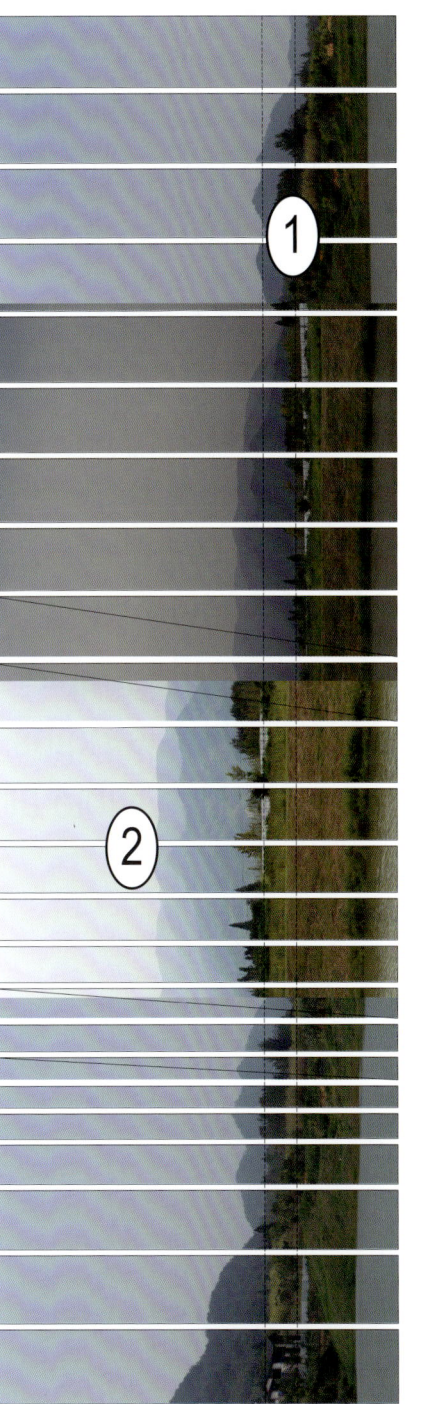

1   The longest bamboo pole available is shorter than what is required for longest bracing elements. Poles can be spliced to increase length, however, each pole tapers from the base to the tip which makes this difficult—the maximum acceptable diameter at foot is 80mm—have students work with craftspeople to find compatible lengths so no stepping is visible at the intersection;

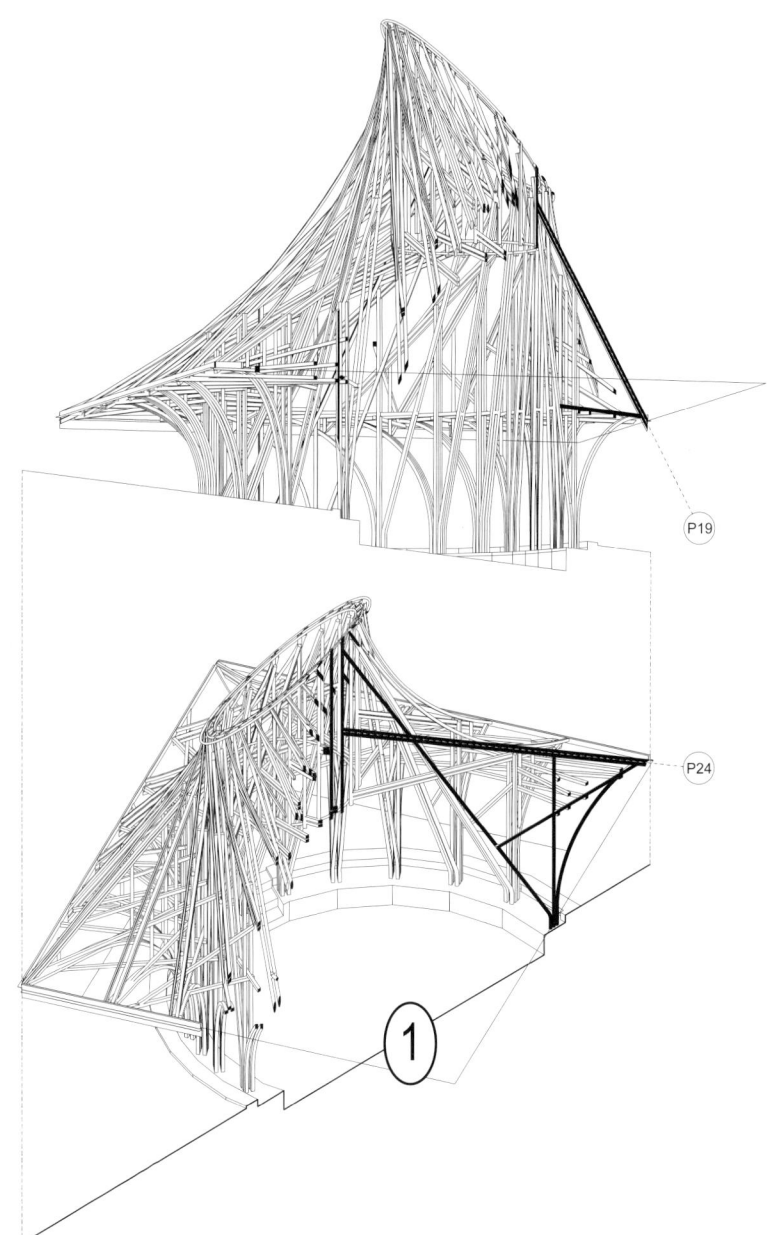

1. Current designed radius unachievable, maximum consistent bending radius of the bamboo pole is approximately 1.8m—adjust on-site;

2. Craftspeople cannot read the drawing with radius and request instead arc length + distance, redraw to match the jig they have constructed on site;

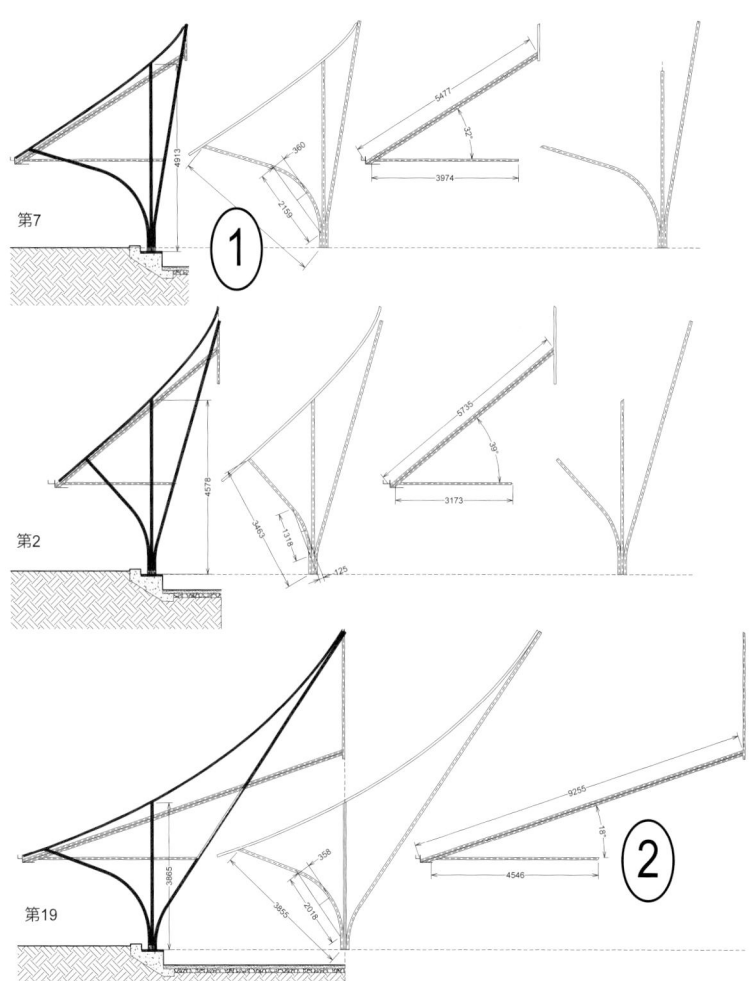

1   Each of the 24 roof sections are double curved, fabric underlay for fiberglass must stretch in both directions. The cotton Elastane blend works best in our tests;

2   The fiberglass resin does not like the cold! Must be complete now before temperature drops otherwise it will not set;

3   Glass fiber matt must be applied carefully to the exterior of the hardened fabric formwork. This must be done with a brush, kept clean, and undertaken in small sections. Remake test strip;

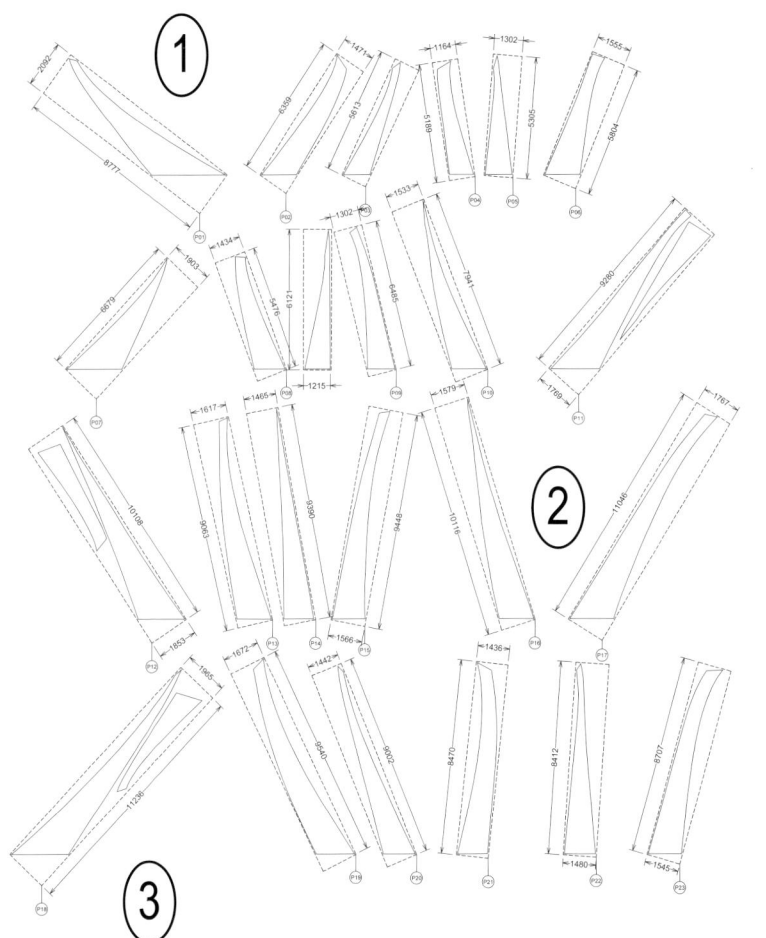

1. The location of pins on oval guide rings are critical! Student team to accompany craftspeople to local pipe bender and to mark locations precisely using the 1:1 print outs. Ring must be galvanized;

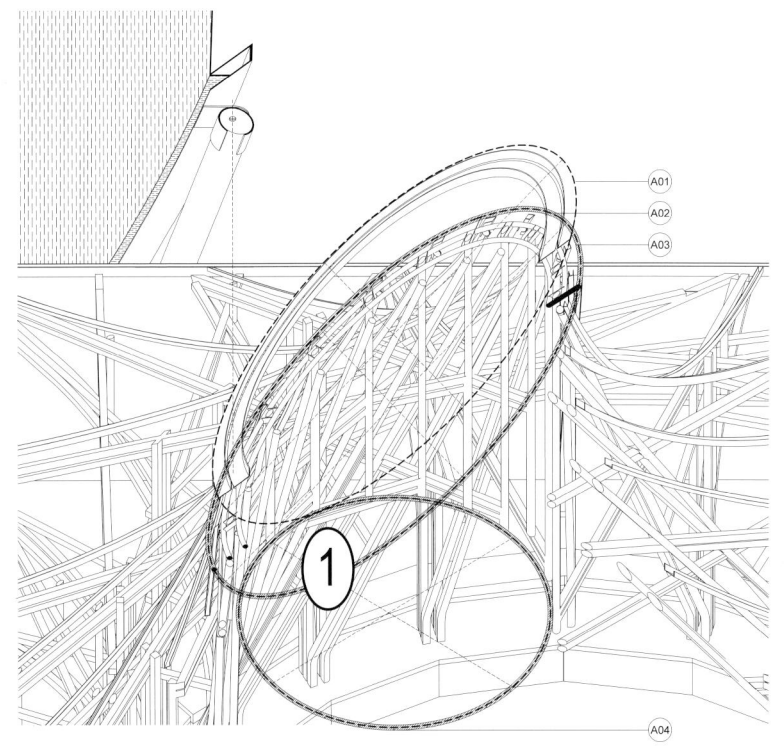

Concrete ring foundation with steel footings for connecting the columns.

Placing the first bay into position after being prefabricated flat onsite.

The changing distances between columns capture the surrounding landscape in a dynamic way.

Tensile roof membrane stretched from square to elliptical profiles.

REDEFINING THE COLLECTIVE: Renovation Strategies for the Ancient *Tulou*

The long history and evolution of the *tulou* (literally earth-house) is itself a story of collective living taking place in the southern and eastern regions of China over the past millennium. As the shape and form of its architecture evolved, it directly mirrored changes in ways of living together. Even as these dense fortress houses first emerged out of an aggressive and hostile environment, within these protective walls, a model of self-reliance and close-knit relationships was forged on a foundation of mutual protection. Individual families were organized without hierarchy—each living in a single vertical stack of spaces divided evenly along the periphery, each responsible for defending their section of wall. The functional programs were organized from the ground up, with kitchens on the first floor, followed by bedrooms and storage under the roof. Along the inside facade of each level is a shared public corridor. Because circulation from floor to floor occurred only at specific points, sometimes with just a single vertical stair—the highly used corridors only enhanced the intertwined aspect of living collectively. These three- to four-story story apartments, arranged around a central void filled with communal activity closely resembles an urban building type, albeit emerging out of a rural context. Seen from the perspective of urban experiments in collective housing from the last century, the *tulou* model remains radical and surprising. As the urban context of China continues to evolve, can these unique and intuitive experiments in community living still enliven us today?

Right: The spaces surrounding the *tulou* buildings are rapidly densifying, leading to a landscape that is neither rural nor urban.

Early on, we visited one large circular *tulou* whose ground floor was subdivided into a series of concentric rings. In the very center was a small temple, a surprising and intimate courtyard in the narrow and seemingly endless maze of corridors. This *tulou* originally functioned as a school—serving the children of neighboring extended families. The inter-relationships and growing connectivity between closely situated but independent structures represent the emergence of an urbanism, unlike the growth of ancient walled towns or cities. Instead of an ever-expanding urban boundary, the *tulou* landscape grew into an unusual rural urban mix, remaining fixedly rooted in the idea of the house. The multiplication of private houses containing public institutions—nonetheless surrounded by open fields of agricultural production is a surprising diagram of urban development. Especially in the simple fact that the idea of collectivity is preserved and strengthened along the lines of growth. Until now.

Today, the landscape surrounding these once dominant buildings has become crowded with concrete-frame houses that can be built much more easily and quickly by the villagers themselves. Having transitioned away from a common livelihood, collective living is less appealing than individual houses. For those that remain in the *tulou*, the transformation is equally stark as the shared central space has become subdivided into a clutter of individual toilets and kitchens. It's evidence that the common good has been subjugated to the desires of the individual. As the surrounding urban fabric densifies, the *tulous* are becoming abandoned. Where once they might have represented an urban typology in the rural, they now seem to be what remains of outdated rural buildings in increasingly urban environments.

It seems reasonable that an architectural solution exists that could balance the necessity for modern comforts with the

Right: New shower and toilet facilities are plugged into the back of the existing *tulou*.

preservation of public amenity. By comparison, the *tulou* has the potential to seem more advantageous than the hyper-dense and unregulated sprawl of urban fabric outside. Fundamentally, it's not a mere transformation in form and construction, but in the balance between individual and collective interest. One of the biggest paradoxes of urbanization and densification is the tendency toward individualization. Yet mediating the common ground; particularly finding added value in the collective agenda is a role that architects are well suited to perform.

Tracing back the long history of the *tulou*, it is evident that a unique concept of urbanization evolved hand in hand from these collective houses. As the population grew, more and more *tulous* dotted the increasingly agrarian landscape and began to share essential facilities. Contained in each central space, the provisions of urban life—schools, marketplaces, temples, hospitals—emerged. The *tulou* retained aspects of private house and public facility. The context was characterized by intensified moments of urban life in patchworks of farmland: A proto-urban condition. This situation that combined intensified urban living in a largely rural setting remains a unique model of urbanization even today.

In our journeys conducting research and design studios over a period of ten years, we began to discover cases of *tulou* adaptation by local inhabitants. Contained in the physical upgrading and transformations of the ancient structures, was an evolution in thinking about the relationship of families and their community. Taken as inspiration, we began to consider what the next stage in the evolution of this building type might be. Could we fully transform the abandoned *tulous* into pubic institutions, repositioning them in the burgeoning towns and cities that now needed them? Together with the Longyan government, an altogether new approach to cultural and historic preservation was conceived—not by conserving these buildings, but in their active re-development. With the government, abandonded *tulous* were selected and analyzed alongside a list of potential programs ranging from libraries, work spaces, marketplaces, schools, or even sports and swimming facilities. The collaboration emphasized the ever-changing and resilient nature of this form of vernacular architecture, hoping to re-establish their role as "everyday" architectures, in contrast to the approach of other historic *tulou* counties.

With a very limited budget, it was important to consider how to make the most effective and focused renovation with the biggest impact. The traditional *tulou* is inhabited by multiple families, but takes the shape of a large house, with a single door and stair inside, unified by the simple geometry of its outer wall. We explored ideas to redefine these structures spatially, and how our interventions might respond to the large-scale forces of urbanization. Not only does this require a careful reading of the overall contextual transformation, but an attempt to re-situate renovated buildings within a new spatial dynamic. Our approach presumes that buildings (vernacular ones in particular) are a result of the complex ecology of a site: this includes the social, economic, political, and environmental conditions that make this way of building possible. By altering the spatial construct of the building, might these buildings open the way for new social and economic relationships?

Two projects were eventually built, testing two opposing strategies of engagement: introversion and extroversion. The Window-Stair redefines the protective outer wall, reinventing a new entry into a second-story window while invigorating the space in front of the wall through a new seating area and performance space. The Stair-Tower on the other hand engages the interior of the *tulou*, activating the public corridor and balconies by connecting them with a free-standing spiral stairway eventually leading to a viewing platform above the roof line. One project responds to an existing renovation by the local villagers while the other anticipates it, being the first act in a longer story of transformation.

The idea of breaking through the wall was not new. In fact the villagers had already begun to do this by "plugging in" a concrete block housing shower and toilet facilities to the back of the structure. This *tulou* had previously been renovated by the villagers into a children's weekend and summer school. Our approach was to engage the front of the *tulou*, highlighting the traditionally small defensive windows. Our prototype introduces a small public library on the second floor, accessible from a new staircase that doubles as a covered seating area facing the farmland. The use of the front courtyard as a performance space is not altogether new—in fact, the most common and important public activity in ancient *tulou* societies was manifested in the form of a theater and stage attached to the front of the *tulou's* outer wall. Our open "room" is a space for reading, resting, or viewing the landscape.

The second project addresses the introverted space of the *tulou*, intensifying the inner courtyard that is so important in providing a sense of collectivity. The project takes place in an abandoned *tulou* and is the first step in the eventual conversion of this structure into a guest house. The organization of individual families in the *tulou* results in each family occupying a vertical stack of rooms. The different floors are accessed by a single shared staircase, often situated over the main entrance door. Open corridors running along the inner courtyard at each floor level lead away from the main stair and allow access to the individual rooms. In going from room to room on the separate floors of a single "home," there is always the chance to run into neighbors and family along all the public hallways and stair. The social life of *tulou* living is intensified through the shared stairway.

Stair-Tower re-organizes the inner courtyard by placing a vertical stair at its center, providing new connections, shortcuts, and an opportunity to climb up to a viewing platform just above

Left: The once collective inner courtyard is often subdivided into independent toilet and kitchen facilities—a takeover by individual interests.

the roof. The collective courtyard has become a multi-layered space. New public programs are introduced along the way as the changing rhythm of the steps allow people to sit, read, or even drink tea inside the tower. Social interactions are predicated by new visual and spatial connections. The new structure radically alters the old building, but is independent of it, creating a new dialogue between old and new. In fact, the stair is designed to be its own scaffolding, building itself while spiralling upward, never relying on the 300-year-old building for support.

Our interest in renovating the *tulou* began with the observation that it was a building form that seemed to be left behind, we began to consider how the architect can participate in the evolution of the vernacular, and how design propositions might lead to the spatial and social evolution of architecture and its context.

The government initially proposed nine *tulous* for consideration, located in a variety of contexts, some buried in dense urban fabric, while others still existed among agricultural farmland. To test if the *tulou* could provide new experiences of collectivity, we tested a variety of strategies engaging different aspects of "house" such as wall, ground, door, stair, corner, tower, roof, window, or corridor. Each proposal experiments with the *tulou* as a form, challenging notions of shape, proportion, opening, density, and height. The *tulou* is at the juncture of a transition from collective to individual, rural to urban. Could its spatial evolution invites new ways to inhabit the *tulou*, translating its inherent collectivity towards a new commons—finding new reasons to live together.

EXAMPLE 3: WINDOW-STAIR

1   Window is the new door! ... Before breaking through the mud wall, check the room inside

2   The hole needs to align with the floor without touching the ceiling;

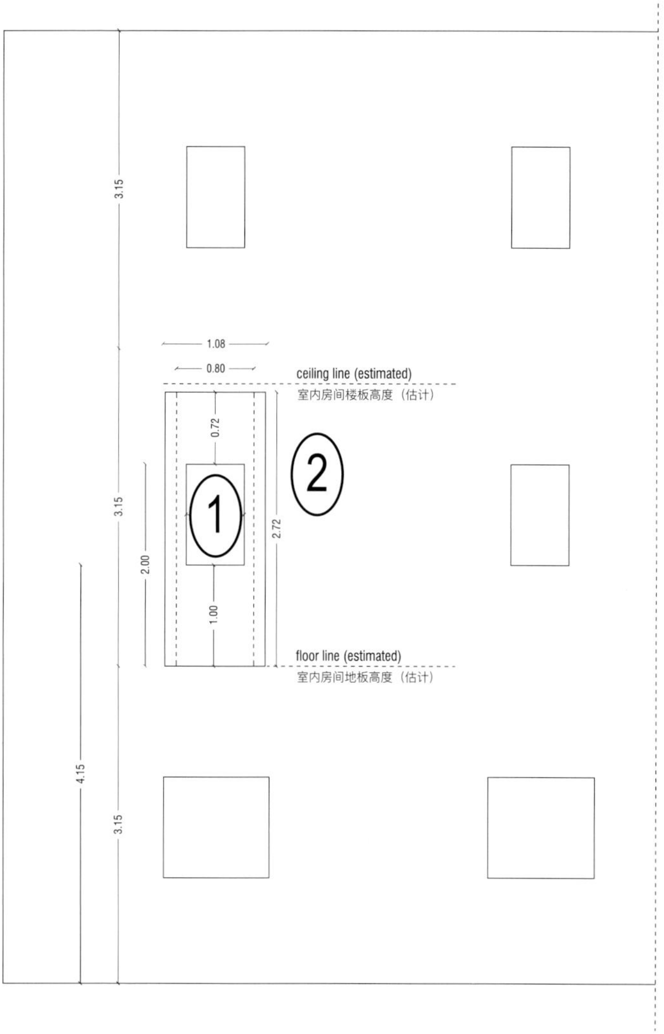

	1.08	
	0.80	

ceiling line (estimated)
室内房间楼板高度（估计）

0.72

① ②

2.72

3.15

2.00

1.00

floor line (estimated)
室内房间地板高度（估计）

3.15

3.15

4.15

1. When both trusses are lifted up, can insert B12, B13, B14;

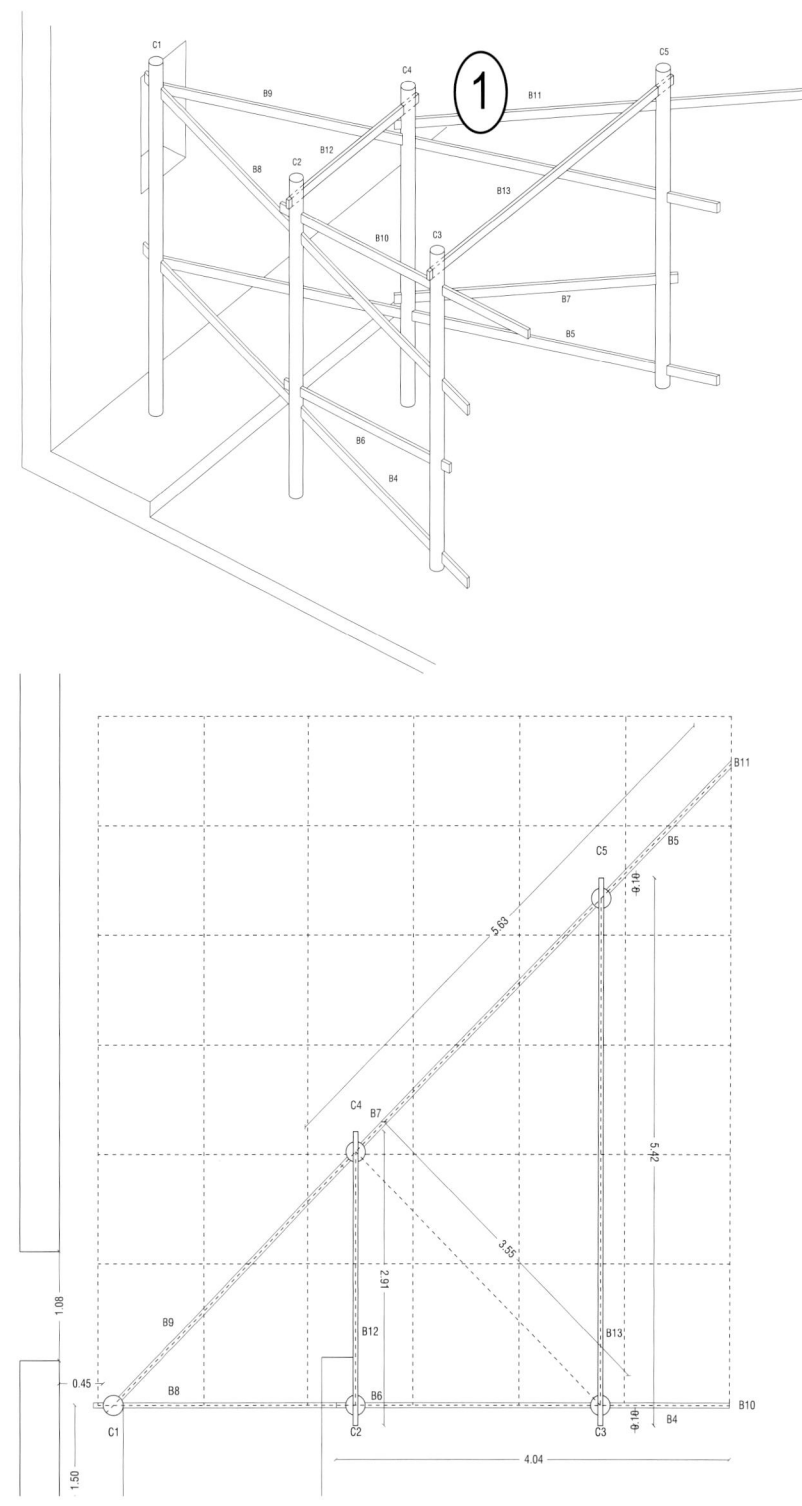

1   Obviously B4 goes all the way through while B8 stops in the middle of C1—check that the beams shouldn't collide!

C1
C2
C3
2.79
4.04
B14
B12
B13
B10
0.20
0.30
2.79
2.79
6.00
5.63
2.35
2.25
2.79
1.45
1.55
B8
5.60
1.10
1.00
2.91
0.10
0.10
B6
1
0.24
0.34
2.58
2.48
1.50
1.60
0.20
0.28
0.18
0.03
B4
0.10
0.45
1.80

8.11
5.65
C1
C5
C4
C2
B14
B13
B12
B11
B9
5.60
6.00
3.95
B7
3.61
B8

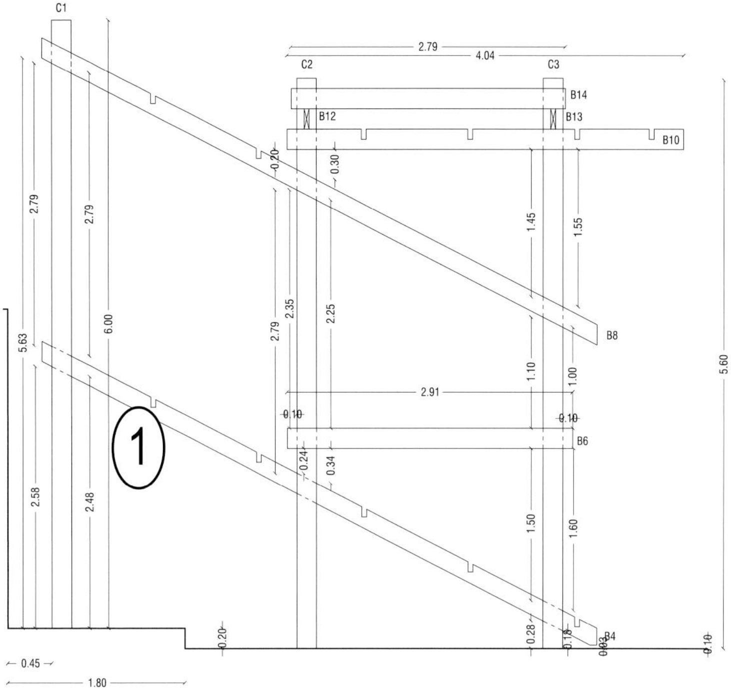

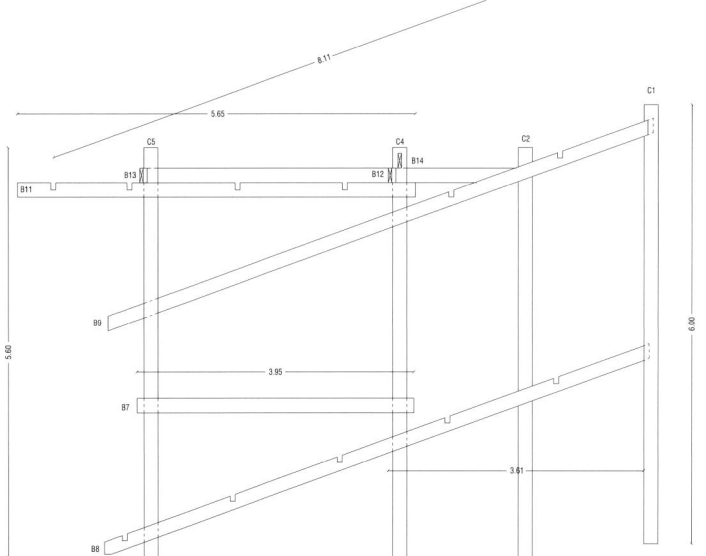

1   Beams sections might change depending on availability—if so, need to mentally adjust measurements on site accordingly;

1
E8a E8b
E7a E7b
E6a E6b
E5a E5b
E4a E4b
E3a E3b
E3c E3d
E4c E4d
E5c E5d
E6c E6d
E7c E7d
E8c E8d
5.02
4.96
4.41
3.87
3.15
2.65
0.10
0.05
tot. n 2
共两根
1.08
0.75
0.91
0.93
0.84
1.04
1.11
1.32
0.86
1.89
2.19
2.98
3.28
4.06
4.36
4.82
5.12
0.61
0.66
E1d
E2c E2d
C1
C2
C3
C4
C5
B4
B5
S2
S3

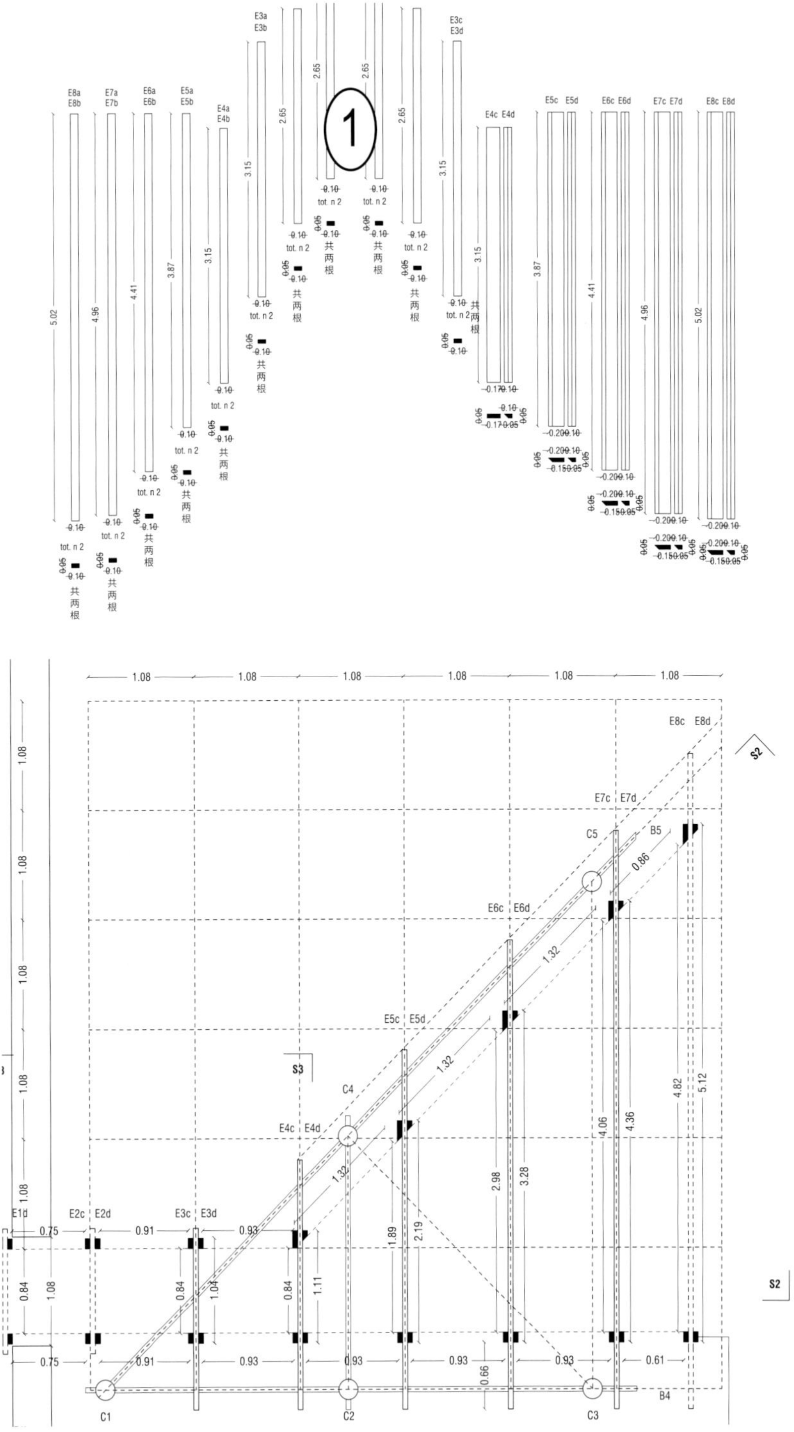

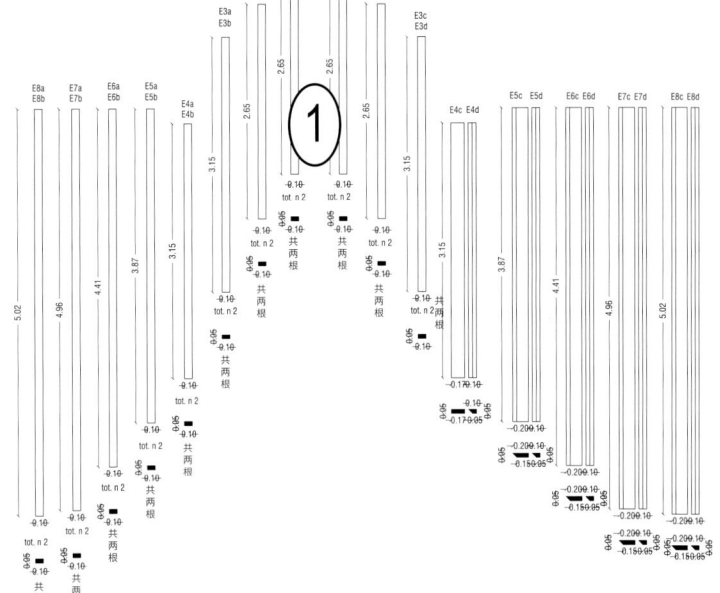

1. Check that cladding of steps is cut precisely to meet cladding of wall;

Beams L vertical 200x50mm

梁 L 50X50mm

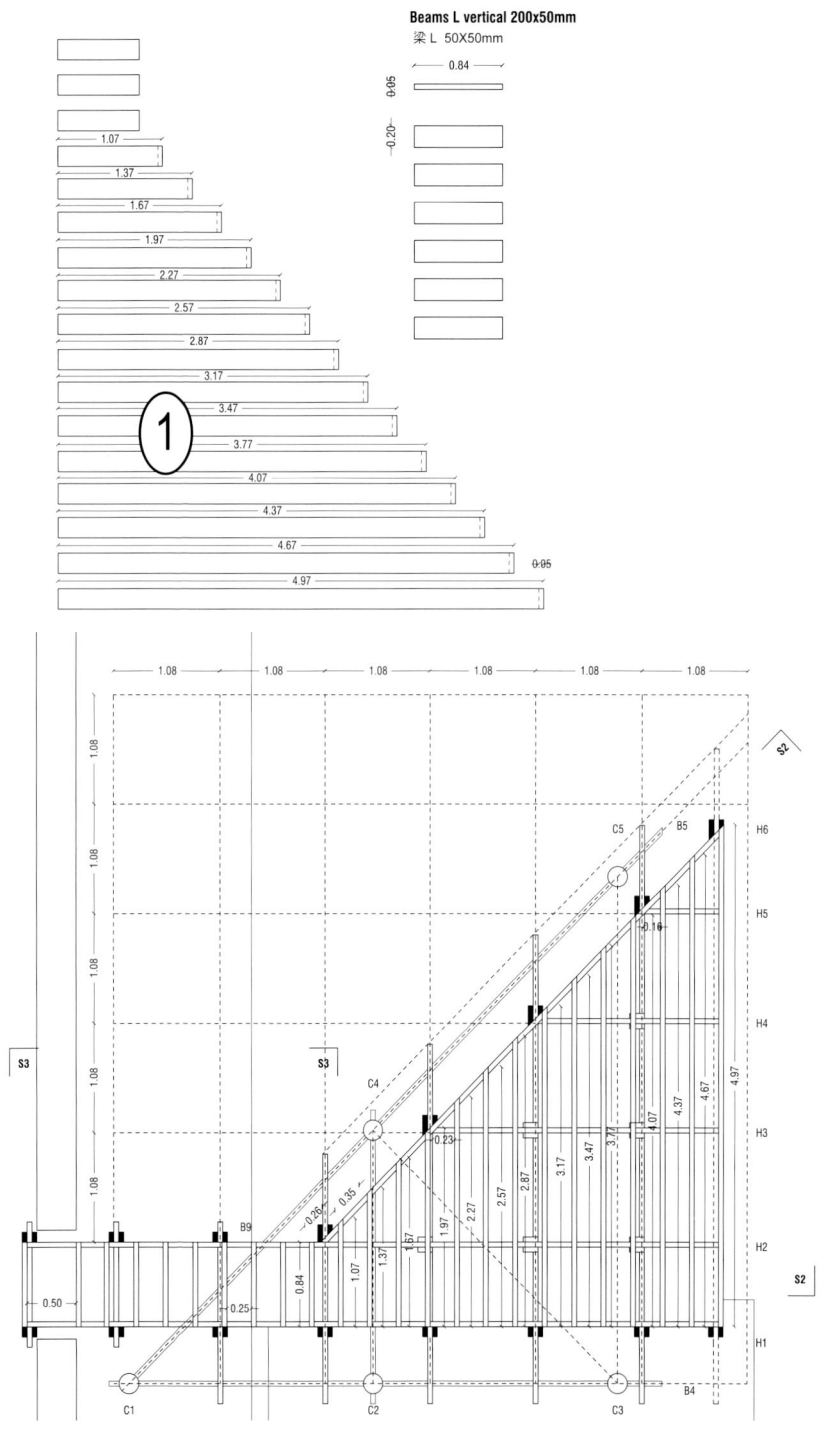

1   Clad the interior so it feels like a box while structure is visible from the outside;

D-t 1
D-t 2
D-t 3
D-t 4
D-t 5
D-t 6
E2b
F2
E3a
E3b
F3
E4a
E4b
F4
E5a
E5b
E6a
E6b
E7a
E7b
E8a
E8b
B11
F5
F6
F7
F8
1
C1
1.01
D-b 1
1.04
D-b 2
C2
1.04
D-b 3
1.04
D-b 4
1.04
C3
B5
D-b 5
0.20
0.42

0.14
0.34
0.54
0.74
0.94
1.14
1.34
1.54
1.74
1.94
2.14
2.34
2.54
2.74
2.94
3.15
7.20
6.60
6.30
6.00
5.70
5.40
5.10
4.80
4.50
4.20
3.90
3.60
3.30
3.00
2.70
2.40
2.10
1.80
1.50
1.20
0.90
0.60
0.30

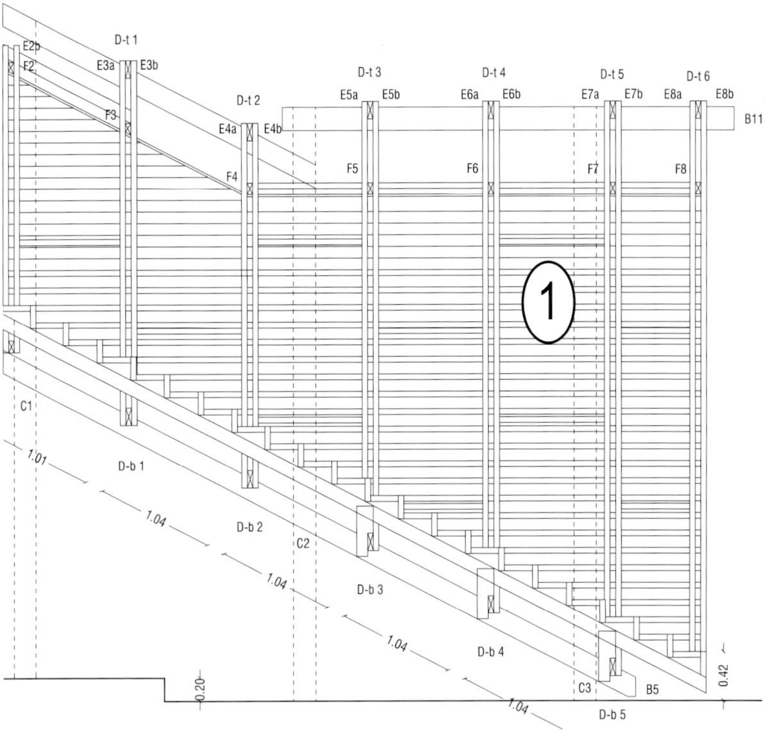

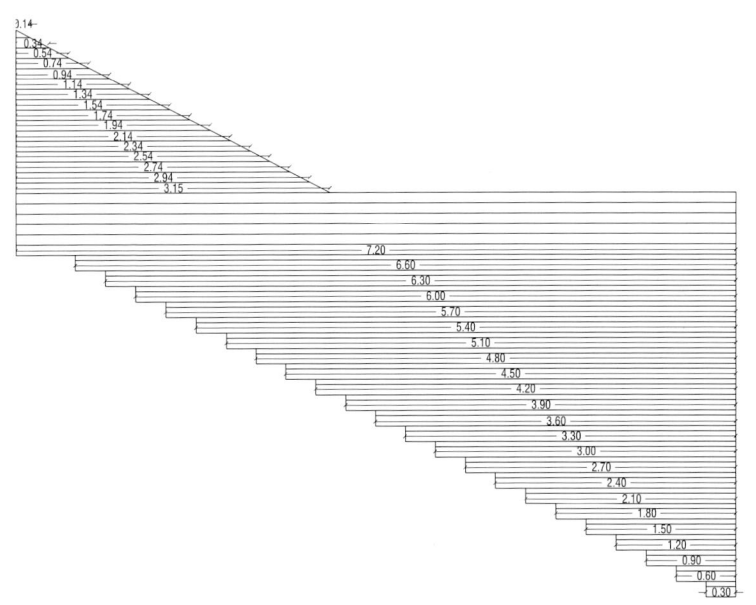

1. If beams sections are different it's okay—the most important thing is that length of F beams MUST NOT change in any case!

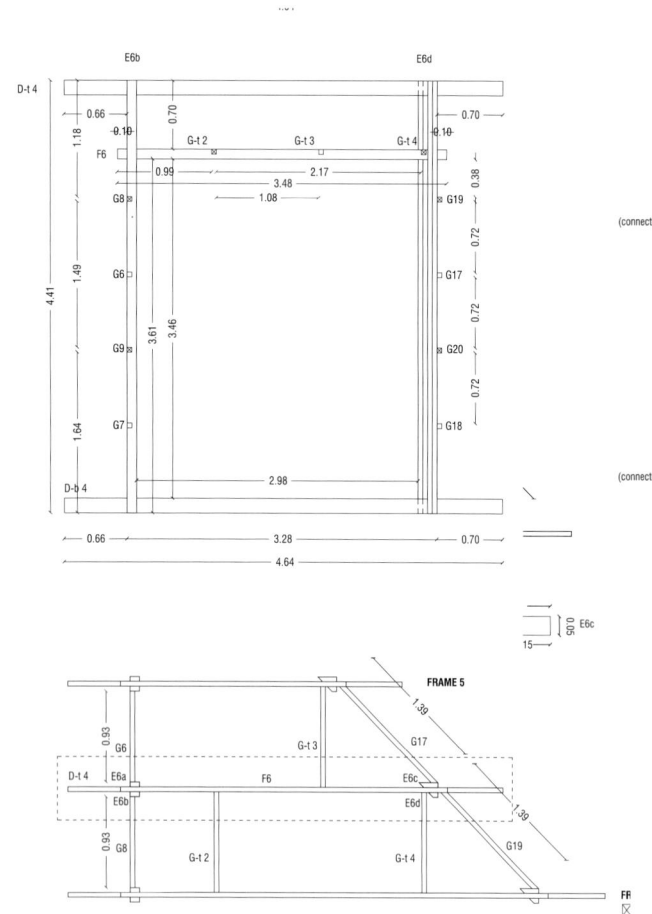

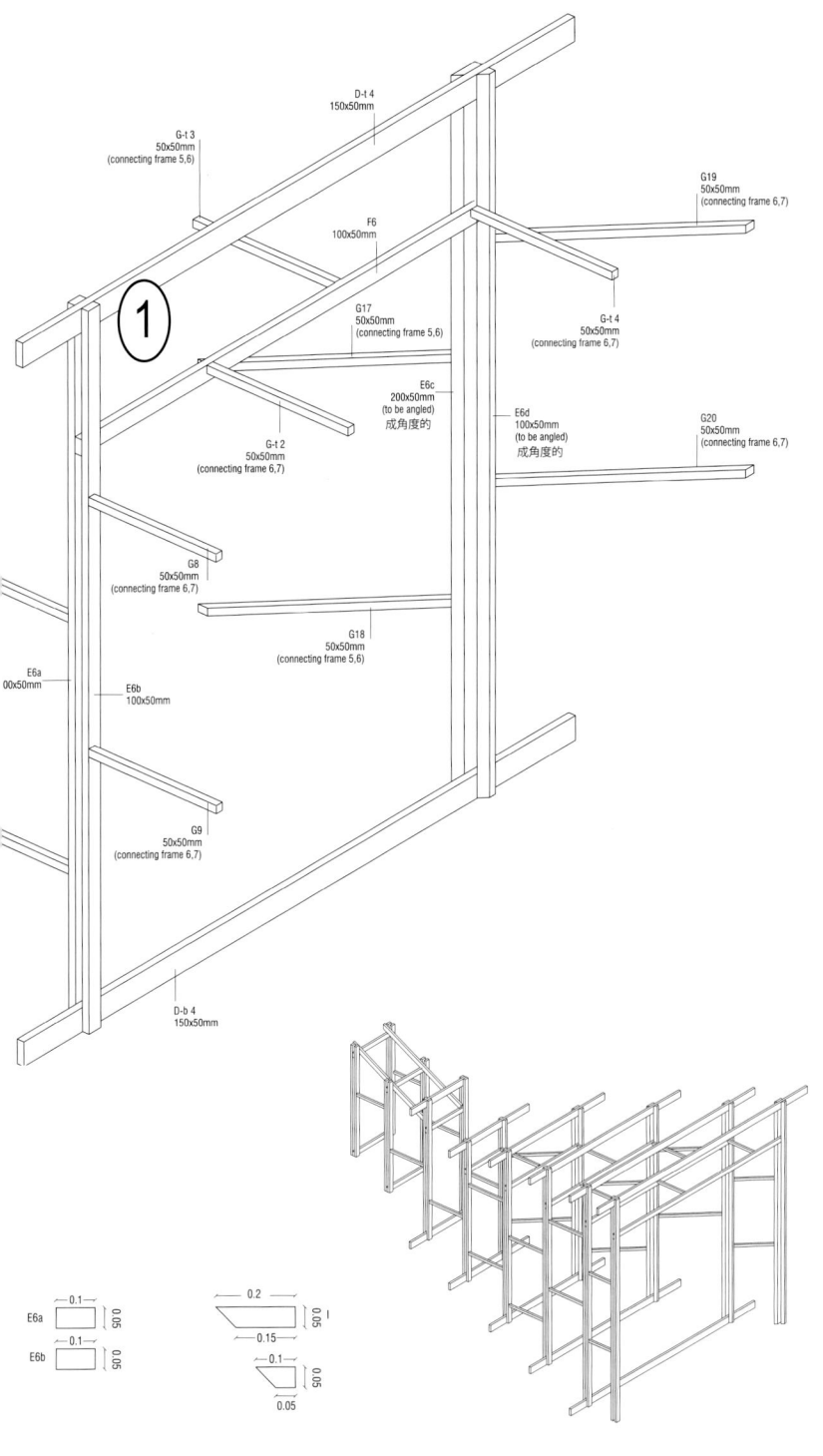

The main trusses of the structure have been laid out and assembled on the ground of the outer courtyard of the *tulou*.

Students measuring and marking the beams according to the construction drawings.

The Window-Stair structure goes through the new door-window without relying on the ancient *tulou*.

EXAMPLE 4:
STAIR-TOWER

1   Not sure about the condition of the existing *tulou*—rooms in every floor to be checked for overall design;

2   The water well on the right to be incorporated in the tower—would be nice to see one well when entering the *tulou* while discovering the other going around the new structure;

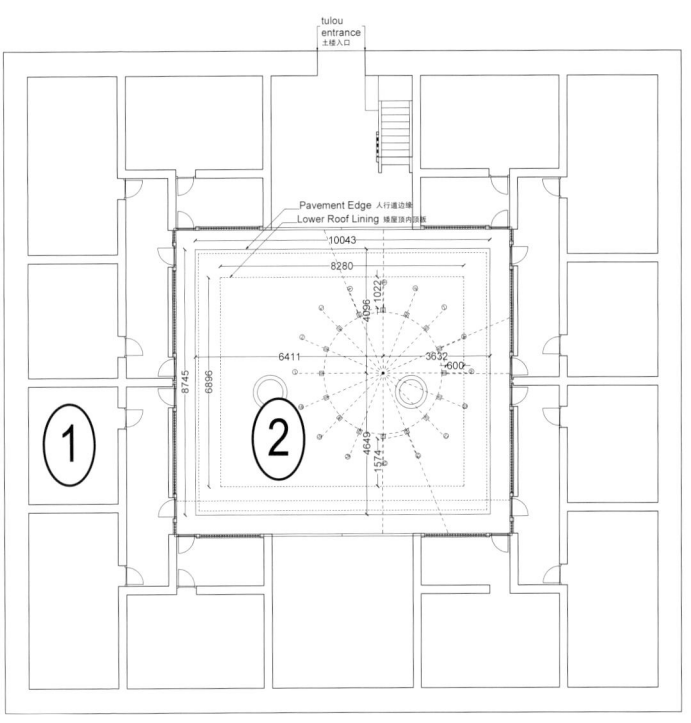

1. We should ask Liu how he plans to do the foundation ring. We can use it as reference for columns' array—they should be attached on the side, not sitting on it;

2. The central columns needs to be notched to allow the beams of the surrounding sixteen columns to pass through—for sure we need two columns, how do we join them together? I would use traditional joints as much as possible;

3. A foundation ring looks better than a slab—need to solve the foundation of the central column. It might look as simple as this;

4. I got an idea: if the courtyard of the *tulou* already has a concrete slab, let's use the existing concrete ground for the foundation!

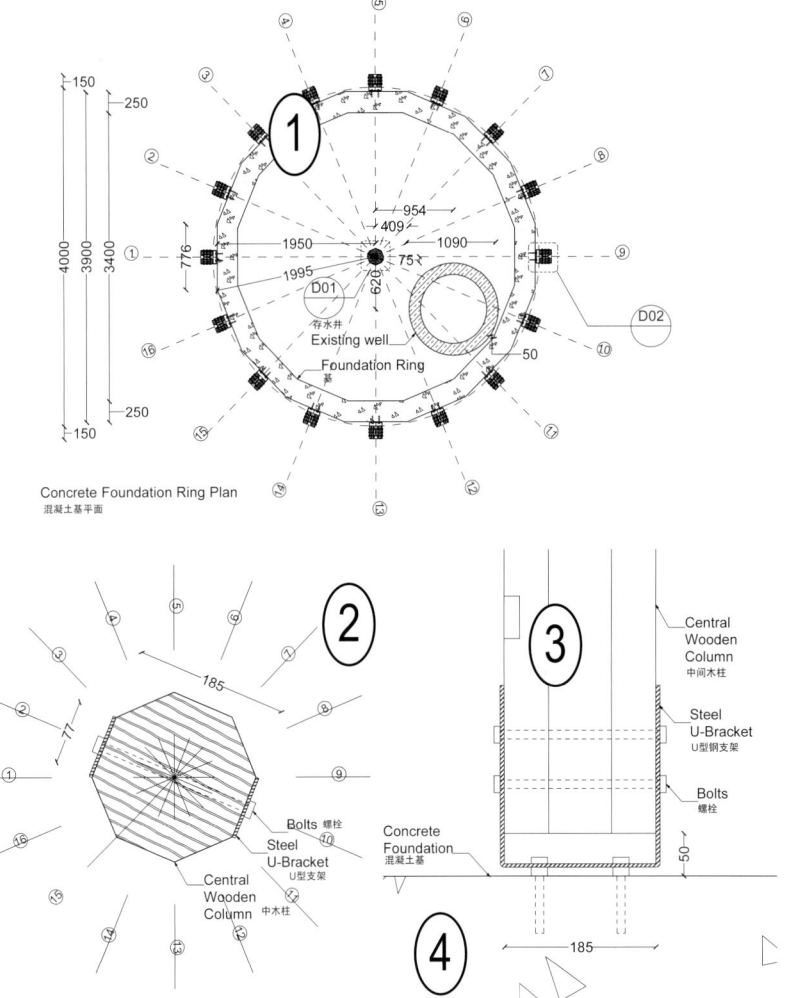

Concrete Foundation Ring Plan
混凝土基平面

1. See this section in relation to the foundation plan
D01 = central column
D02 = outer columns

2. Proposal of connection of outer columns—foundation ring. We should test anyway how deep the existing concrete ground is!

3. Check with contractor availability of steel brackets;

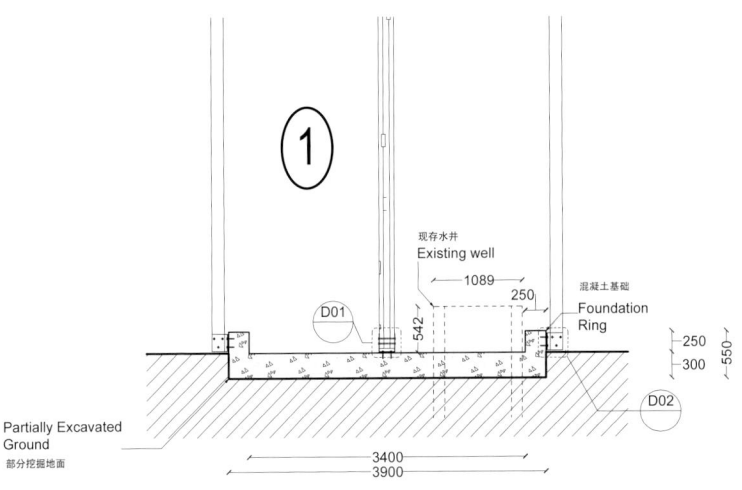

Concrete Foundation Section
混凝土基础剖面

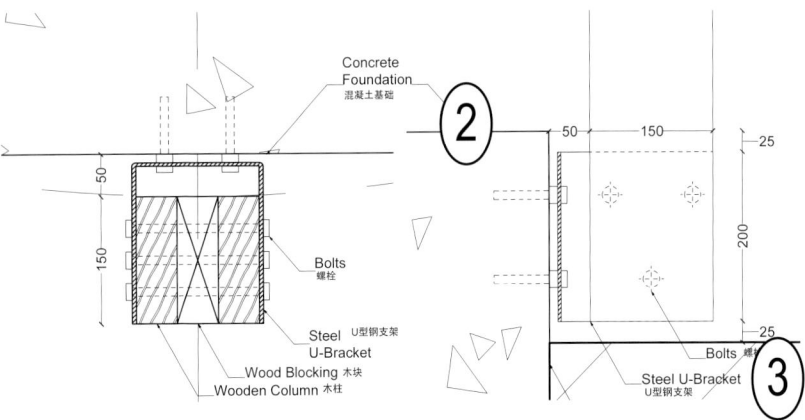

1   Bracing of columns to be tested—do we want a specific pattern?

2   We can keep it as simple as this. The section of bracing beam depends on what's available—we can use leftovers as long as they are all the same size;

3   This elevation will be useful for students—always need to double check marking on columns;

4   Max. distance (vertical) between bracing beams: 1,900mm—from ground: 2,985mm; Min. distance: 530mm

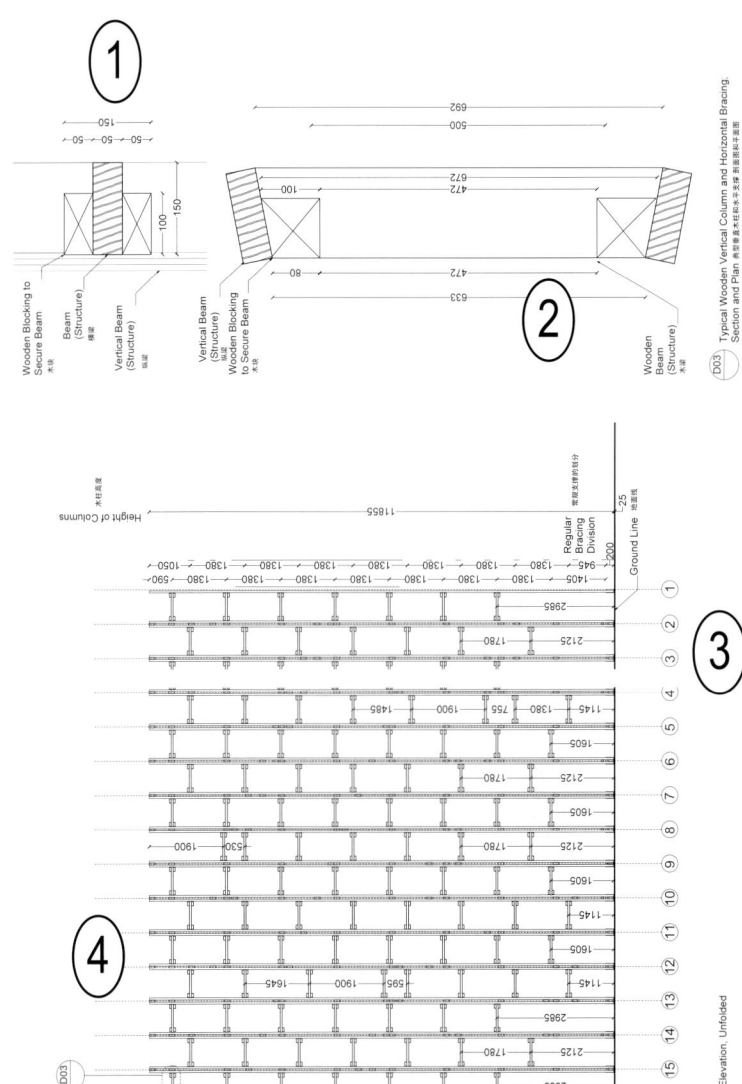

1. Ideally we would shape the central column this way—but since they are two and must be jointed, either it's down perfectly or we keep them round section;

2. All beams' dimensions based on Liu's estimate—keep in mind that sections will likely change. Drawings to be adjusted accordingly;

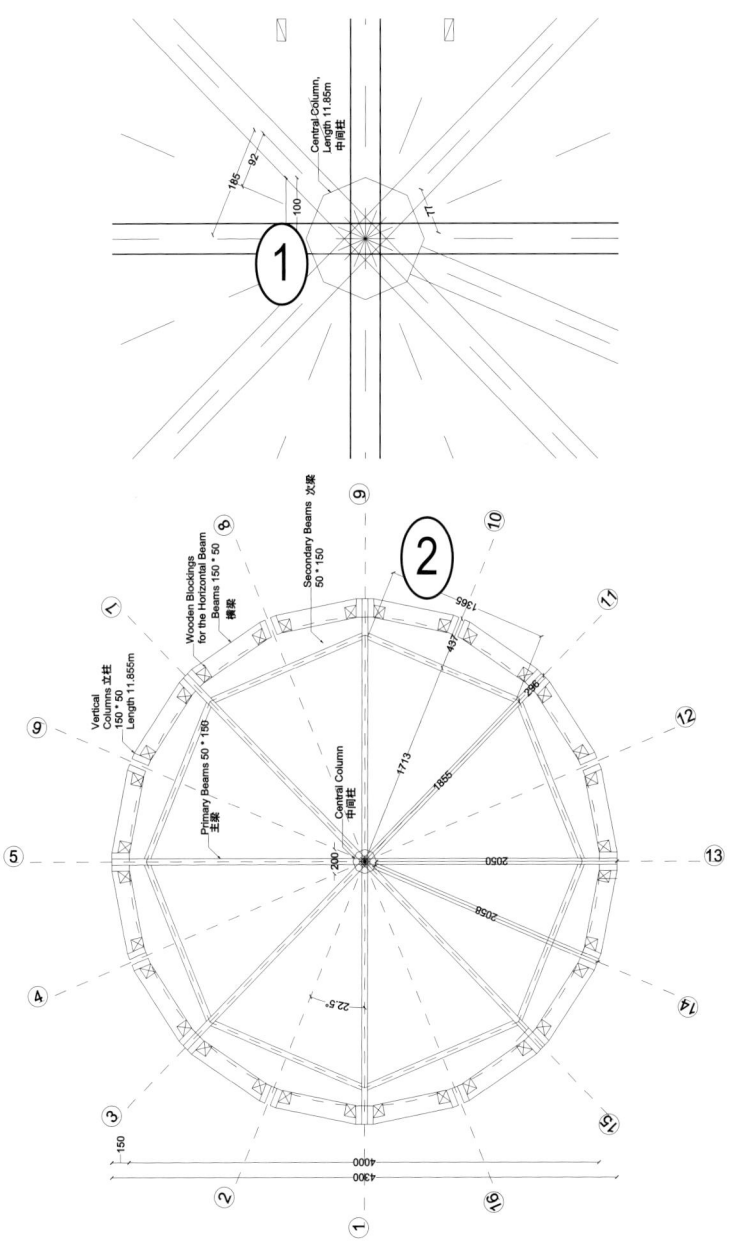

1. We can have a group of students preparing step beams since the beggining—make sure they LABEL everything!

2. There is always a big step, medium step, small step. When labelling them, always reference column number and height from the ground!

3. No need to worry about decking—but make approximate calculation of how many boards needed when on site;

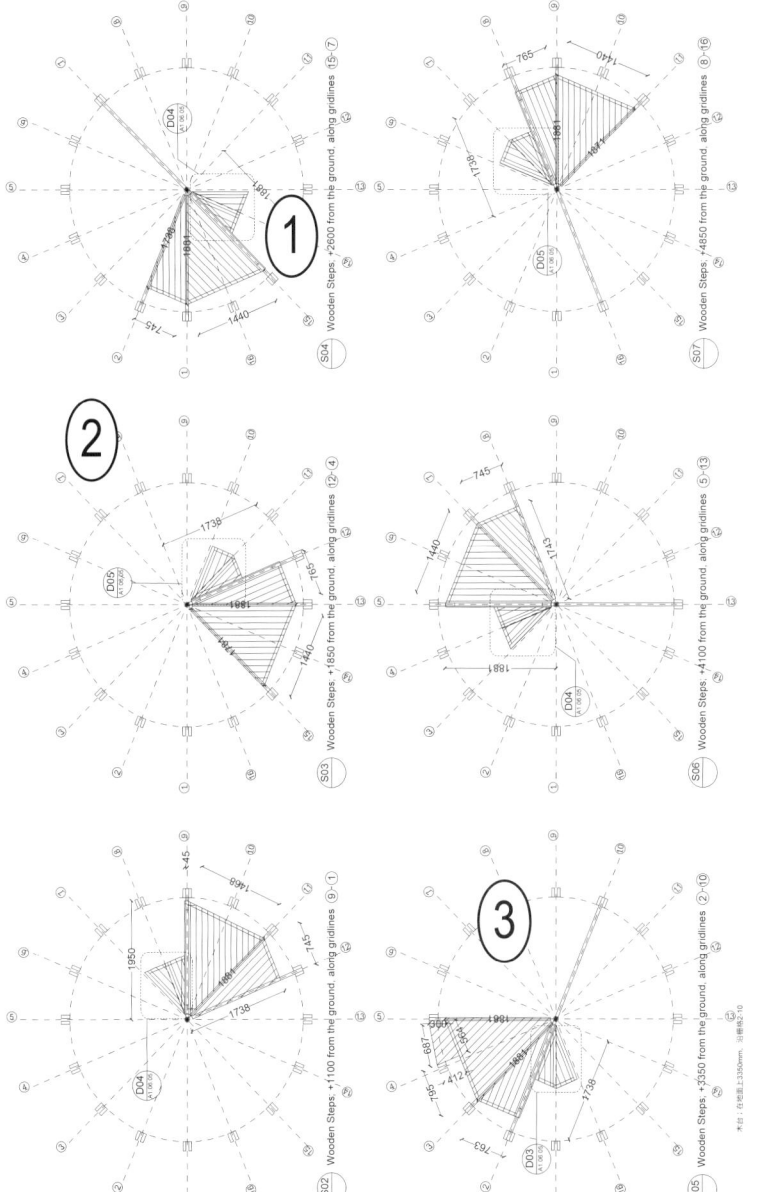

1. To be decided: How does decking meet central column? Does it touch it? Do we leave a space? If so, hole must be smaller than a child's foot;

2. Steps on steps should feel solid: Boards covering the height to be calculated on site;

3. Decking pattern follows steps orientation: see if very small boards make sense or not—can be adjusted;

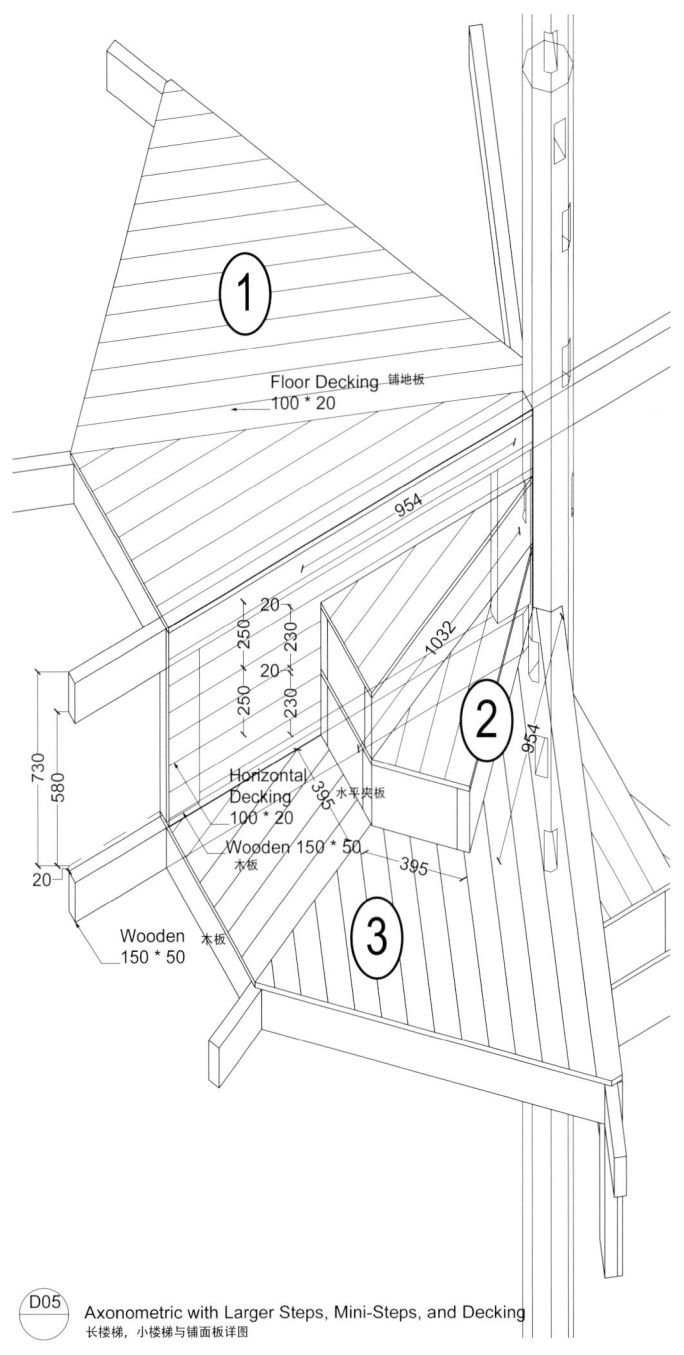

D05 Axonometric with Larger Steps, Mini-Steps, and Decking
长楼梯，小楼梯与铺面板详图

1   Tower connects every floor through the courtyard! Need to check condition of existing corridors to decide location of bridges;

2   The bridges touch the existing structure but DOES NOT rely on it! Tower is completely independent from the *tulou*;

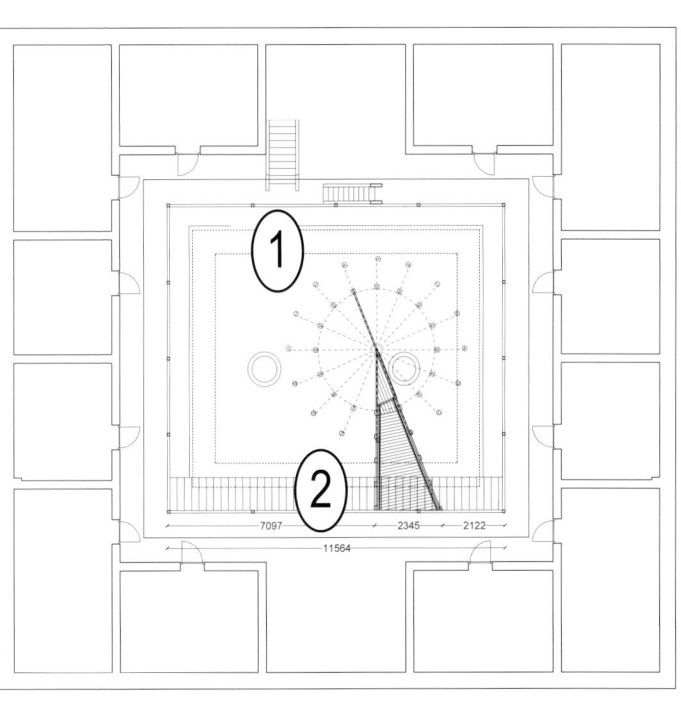

1   Wooden bridges—MOST DELICATE PART! Need to consider how to sit on structure; load needs to be transferred back to the tower; if there is any existing overhanging roof at each floor, need to remove tiles and cut through it;

2   Let's clad the decking on the inside—show structure on the outside;

3   Indicative length of wooden beams for bridges' structure—for sure it will need to be adapted to existing condition;

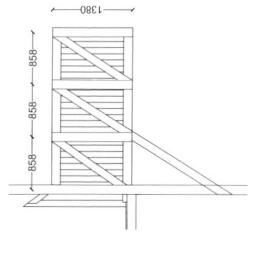

B01 Bridge to First Floor_Elevation
连接一层的桥立面图

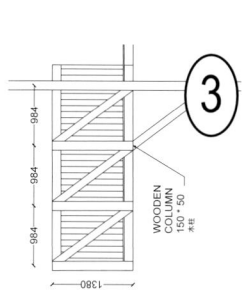

B02 Bridge to First Floor_Elevation
连接一层的桥立面图

1. Need to decide how we finish the top part of railing—simply a beam? decking wrapping around? This can be very last minute decision;

2. Railing follows steps: Keep same language of steps so from the inside the decking feels like a continous skin, while on the outside we show the structure;

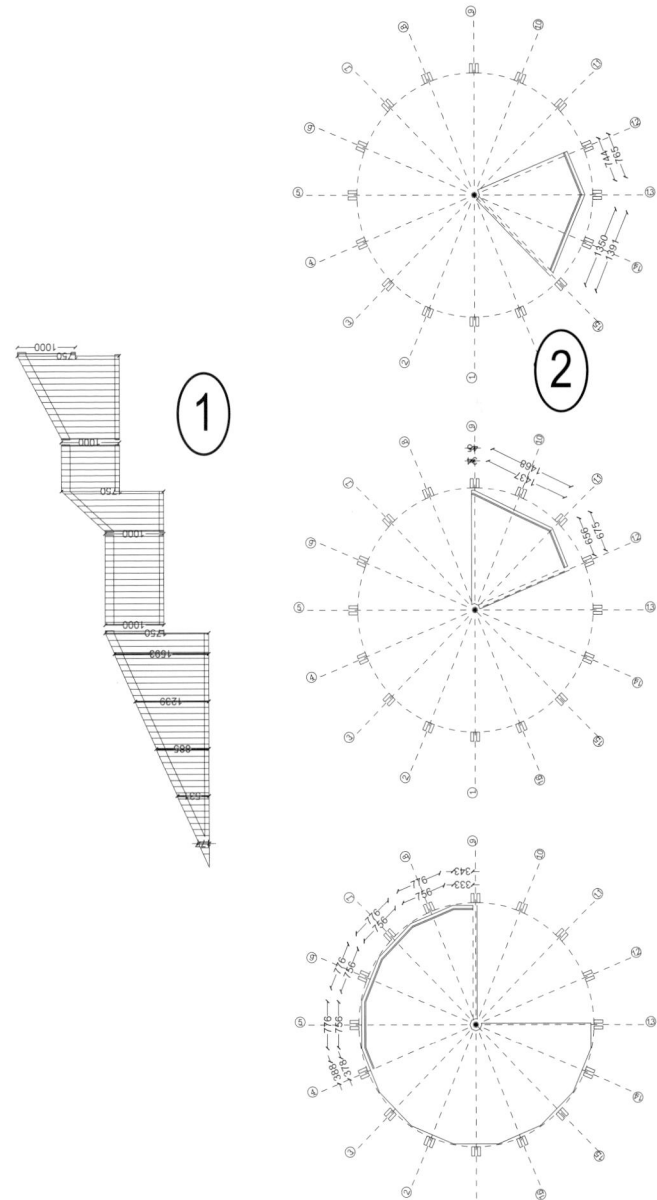

The Stair-Tower is conceived as a self-standing structure that spirals up to the sky from the center of the ancient *tulou*.

The central column has been first notched with traditional techniques and then lifted in place in the inner courtyard of the *tulou*.

The beams of the stairs go through the central beam spanning from opposite outer columns.

The three bridges are the only points of contact between the tower and the *tulou*. They rest on the vernacular structure without transferring any load to it.

TRANSLATING CRAFT
by Donn Holohan

It is often easy to underestimate the pervasive impact of the tools we use. In shaping our tools, we in turn are shaped by them. Whether they are material or more abstract, our tools change the way we feel, act, and think, and can transform how we relate to the world around us. Architects both understand and construct their world through the device of the plan and section; engineers through the balance of reciprocal forces; and craftspeople through tacit material affinities. Caught within our own individual disciplinary feedback loops we can become inured to the qualities and perspectives embedded within the tools of other practices and cultures. In this context, there is a tendency to assign values to our tools: describing them hierarchically as better or worse.

It is perhaps too simplistic to see the evolution of our tools as a linear one. The plotter does not, in fact, supersede the pen; they are different tools, and although they can be used to achieve the same ends, they also offer clearly distinct opportunities. The changing nature and form of the tools we construct are therefore more appropriately framed in terms of a branching continuum, a set of unique potentials rather than a process of obsolescence and replacement.

This is not a widely held position: across a developing China, the ongoing and rapid reconstruction and development effort taking place can be seen as an antagonistic process—a conflict between old and new, tradition and modernism, conservatism and progress. This is the context for an ongoing project located in the remote mountain village of Peitian, situated in China's southern Fujian Province. This work takes

Right: A bespoke kit of parts; columns and beams are shaped, planed, and jointed before being left to fully "season" prior to assembly.

the form of a series of modest architectural interventions and can been seen as an attempt to reconcile the contested territories outlined above; to read, interpret, and translate specific traditional cultures of making through the application of new tools, models of construction, and forms of representation.

Within the ancient settlement of Peitian a new village is being constructed, one which draws its foundational principles from the assembly lines of Ford's Detroit, Le Corbusier's "Wohnmaschine," and Walter Gropius's radical construction kits, rather than its own vernacular traditions. This new architecture is one defined by simplicity, speed of construction, productivity, cost, and certainty. It is a uniform construction that demands a uniformity of materials. It is steel frame, reinforced concrete and glass, not because of any innate quality possessed by these materials, but due to their affordability, ease of mass production, and the simple tools and processes required in their assembly. It is a system of construction and a design language informed and enabled by the automated machine tool.

This new tool, and the places it has defined, now considered normative, can also be seen as polemical to the building cultures and traditions that for thousands of years shaped the unique structures and spaces of the original village. While sometimes dismissed as nostalgic, this existing vernacular is potentially as systematic and as capable as its modernist counterpart despite being founded on very different principles. Rather than an assembly of discrete, uniform, and interchangeable parts designed for mass production, it is instead a sophisticated relational framework in which the dimensions of each building component are codified, not determined.

This difference is perhaps best articulated through an examination of brick construction. Typically, the length, width, and depth of a standard brick is fixed. This uniformity allows for high productivity and unmatched cost effectiveness. However, in order to create sharply curving walls, irregular angles or junctions, or other non-orthogonal features, we need a "special brick"—one which is capable of transforming an orthogonal system at specific moments. Both the standard brick and the brick special are modular elements, however, each follows a disparate imperative; a system of brick specials enables a high degree of specificity and adaptability, however, it comes with an increase in cost and time, resulting from a more complex production process, whereas a system employing only standardized bricks allows for rapid and inexpensive manufacturing and assembly, but can lead to generic, unresponsive, and characterless buildings.

The traditional systems of Peitian are "special" systems. While the number and type of building components is limited, their dimensions, relationships, and quantities remain flexible. Mathematical formulae are used to generate the specific proportions of each component, in which are embedded fundamental construction logics, for example: the span to depth ratio of beams informs the ideal sizing of the tenons incised in those beams, which then informs the resultant column height and diameter required. Even the arrangement and organization of rooms and spaces are ordered and connected in such a way: adjusting any element within this framework forces a transformation of the entire system, which then accommodates those changes within its prescribed limits. This results in a widely applicable and efficient mode of construction that can absorb the variability of regional materials and the idiosyncratic demands of individual communities.

The Peitian approach to making is exemplified and embodied in the Gao-chi (篙尺)—an essential measuring tool on which is inscribed the lengths and proportions of all the elements of a typical structural system. Made for a specific building, each device is unique and is informed by the nature of a given site, the demands of the patrons, and the disposition of the master carpenter who constructs it. It generally takes the

form of long wooden or planed bamboo pole with four, six, and eight faces; each of which is inset with a series of carefully lined and annotated graduations. The Gao-chi works as both a jig for accurately defining the position and level of elements for the construction work and a replacement for architectural drawings. This is a decidedly parametric approach to building, in which the designer's focus is not the modules that make up a system but the definitions of the relationships between them.

The tools favored by the village carpenters in enacting these protocols further supports this mode of construction: the adze, plane, chisel, sash saw, and ink line have no intrinsic memory, meaning that in using each of these tools, the carpenter's hand is unconstrained—he or she relies on embodied skills to accurately fashion each element. Every piece is therefore subtly different. Again, the focus is not on accuracy, but relationships. Each joint must fit tightly; fractional differences between the as-made and the as-drawn are irrelevant. In contrast, industrial machines have a singular focus—each is designed for a specific task: to produce a standardized component in which assembly tolerances are predetermined. These accuracies are secured by complex armatures that constrain the motion of the body in relationship to the tool—ensuring precise repeatability. One tool system finds its advantage in adaptability, the other in ubiquity.

The clash between these two ideologies is apparent and jarring, and to work in this material and ideological context is to maneuver between these two distinct poles. It prompts us away from zero-sum thinking and asks us to consider how new tools and technologies might engage with regional building cultures in new ways, and how each might fundamentally change the other. This process of synthesis disrupts the framing of

Right: A well-worn, six-sided Gao-chi, planed from a single bamboo pole. The dimensions and markings inscribed on its surfaces are specific to a particular building and represent the architecture's design DNA.

architectural technology in terms of linear and incremental improvement.

What if the Gao-chi itself could become a building component, a fragment through which the overall form of the structure is suggested and, through its design, provide a set of instructions to realize that form? This construction would, like the Gao-chi itself, contain the essential intelligence of a design scheme while providing, by nature of its incompleteness, an invitation for reinterpretation by the craftsperson in-situ. Such a device could be made to reflect the culture, crafts, and materials of a specific place and could help to negotiate a collaboration between the hand and the machine, the variable and the known. Using the precision of the machine to empower not overwrite more traditional modes of making could help to elevate these crafts rather than extinguish them.

Further, would it be possible with regard to the means and materials available on site to augment, improve, and make accessible to those less skilled the traditional tools and processes mastered by Peitian's carpenters; critically simplifying and systematizing production? Could this be achieved while increasing the comprehensiveness of the overall design scheme—allowing for the integration of building services and optimizing structural and environmental performance through computational models? This would not be done with the intent of competing economically with the generic ready-made building component but would be a first step toward demonstrating sustainable alternatives.

Wind and Rain Bridge is the first of these experiments—a post-flood reconstruction that provided a clear brief but also a definitive structural and material requirement. In this iteration, the initial focus centered on existing traditional tools and workflows and their transformations. Working between the village and the research laboratories of the University

Right: Each of the bridge's elements is unique, and each joint is fractionally differentiated—a specific response to the site but also a test case.

of Hong Kong, the design for the bridge was shaped in parallel with the making of a set of precision tools that were prefabricated and shipped to the carpenter's workshops. These devices constituted the primary form of instructions issued by the design team to the craftspeople, effectively replacing construction drawings.

The key element of this toolset—a mechanical saw guide and a simple notation—enabled the rapid setting out and cutting of a new type of wood joint. Derived from a complex wedged-stop bladed scarf joint (see 151) found in Peitian's larger, public buildings, this new variant is employed to simplify the process of joining beams end-to-end, increasing their ability to span longer distances.

This relatively particular joint is a product of a material limitation. The village is surrounded by a fast-growing pine—a resource managed by the local community. Although light weight and easily worked, the material is limited in its application, due to both its small section sizes and short lengths. Historically, this has defined the local architecture, in which the dimensions of typical structural bays relate to the maximum length and width of the timber available and, in general, range between three and five meters. Longer spans, such as that which would be required for the bridge, are avoided despite their utility—the joints needed, while elegant, are difficult to make. The tools designed and produced at the university attempt to change this paradigm, simplifying fabrication and enabling a new, less constrained architecture to evolve.

On reflection, while effective in achieving the aims of the project, such a methodology can lead to questions of agency. Arguably, in this instance, the work of the carpenters has been reduced to a form of efficient automation, albeit a

Right: Crating models for site. All models constructed for Sun Room are procedurally, materially, and dimensionally precise—they are not abstractions, but on-site tools.

human-powered one. If the making of new buildings is to be considered not only as a necessary toil, but as useful and fulfilling work, then this method of optimization alone falls short in addressing the loss of a culture of craft.

Sun Room—a shelter for local farmers in Peitian's agricultural landscape, built shortly after the construction of the bridge—attempts to find a compromise between the necessary forms of control required in realizing structural, environmental, or spatial performance and a process of making that allows for discovery and some freedom of individual expression.

Bamboo weaving, the primary material of the pavilion, resists automation. Intricate and sculptural, this craft once widely practiced in the village is in severe decline: just one master remains in Peitian and the originally utilitarian vessels and screens he produces are now marketed to tourists as mementos. It is not that the inherent material intelligence of this practice has been superseded—woven bamboo is light, strong, and materially sustainable—it is rather that it cannot be mass manufactured without a significant loss of quality. In the design of Sun Room, a mode of building is sought which can incorporate this practice, efficiently, without that loss.

The pavilion is designed as a loom: a pair of solid steel rings, held apart in tension by a wooden frame (see 169). The rings define the geometry of the shelter's skin, which is tightly controlled. This is a necessary discipline, as embedded within these elements are the results of both a computational environmental analysis and a consideration of the protected viewsheds that cut through the landscape.

A single, flat packed, prefabricated node determines the set out of the building's structural elements. This concentration and miniaturisation is simultaneously necessitated by the dimensional limits of the postal service and enabled by the high degree of precision offered by computer-controlled

Left: Initial failures—relearning the craft of bamboo weaving with the last craftsperson working in Peitian.

machine tools. This node communicates, controls, orders, and sequences the construction process, however, while its use is specific it is not prescriptive—the node accommodates material variations and absorbs errors. The weaving and interpolation of the bamboo skin is left to the craftsperson's skill. The node is not only a building component but also a precision tool and, while it is a product of an automated process, it is designed to provide a framework rather than a straitjacket, to integrate rather than supersede, thereby enabling the craft process to evolve through synthesis rather than be erased.

In each iteration and revisiting of the village, and with each new tool examined, understood, and re-engineered, new opportunities for this synthesis are presented. This is perhaps the greater part of the legacy of China's rich craft heritage and its potential. While less visible than the physical remnants of ancient structures nestled between modern developments, the devices that were made to realize them are perhaps more important and made further so by their slow dissolution into obscurity.

In contrasting new and old it is easy to dismiss traditional ways of making as regressive or as embryonic forms of our current advanced cyber-physical systems. However, embedded and distilled within even seemingly simple tools are both sophisticated networks of material and culture, and alternative versions of the built environment. The tools and procedures of the carpenters working in Peitian exemplify this and embody a subtle challenge to our current modes of making. It is a practice which is specific rather than generic, it is pragmatic but not utilitarian, local rather than global, and, importantly, it produces an architecture deeply connected with its place, its landscapes, and with its people.

EXAMPLE 5:
WIND AND RAIN BRIDGE

1   The section size has been reduced as discussed—
and the majority of building elements are now no longer than 3.5 meters. However, some of the columns are almost 5 meters in length. Can you talk to the forester to check if he can find something suitable on the hill? If so,
we would need to cut it now! So that it can be seasoned properly. Does he have quota remaining on his license?

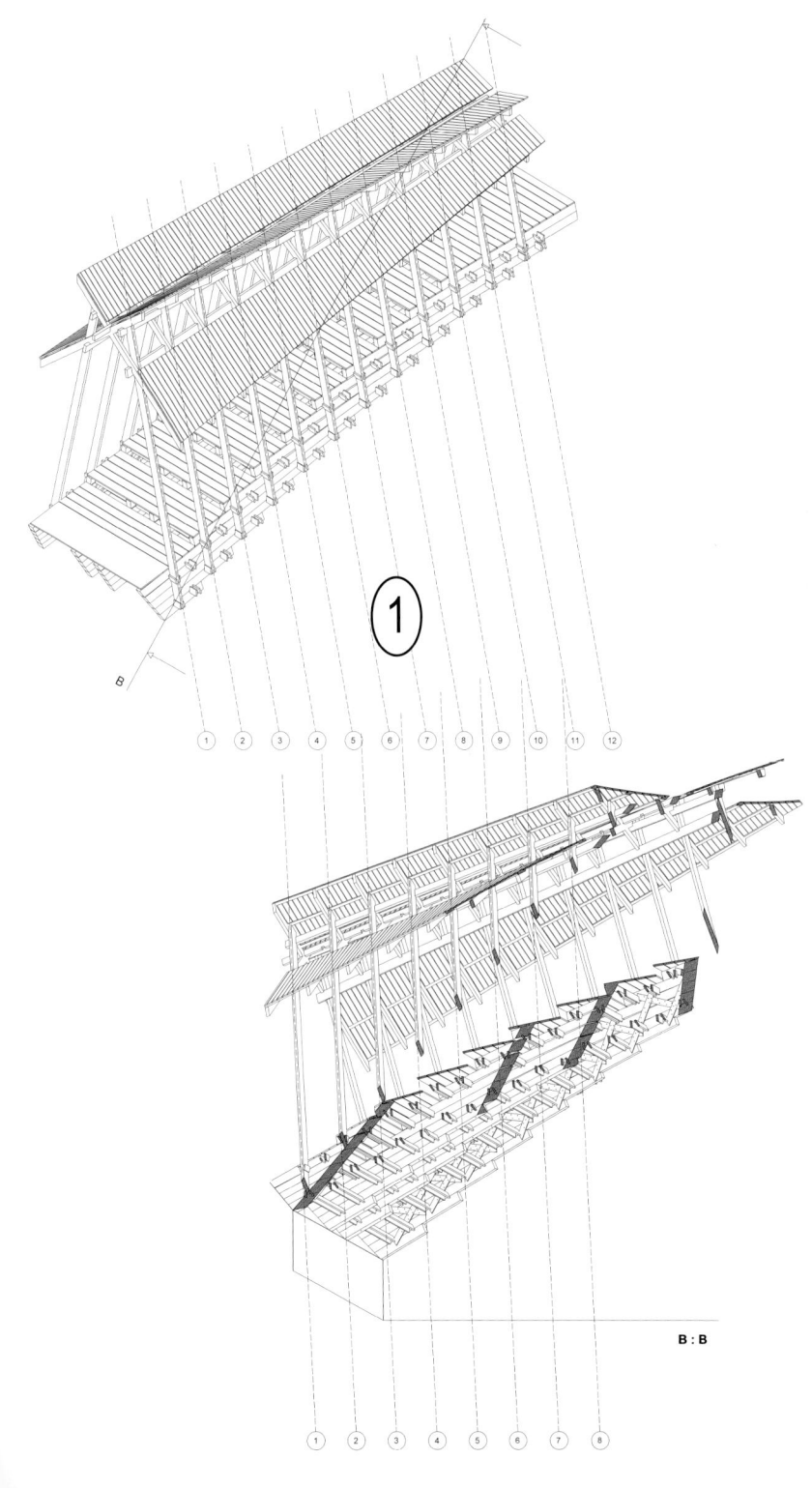

1. Youai, it is critical we use dry not green timber for this project, we will need to season the wood in the workshop over the winter (MC 18% Okay). When bridge is installed over the river the timber will swell and joints will stiffen—we do not want the reverse to happen!

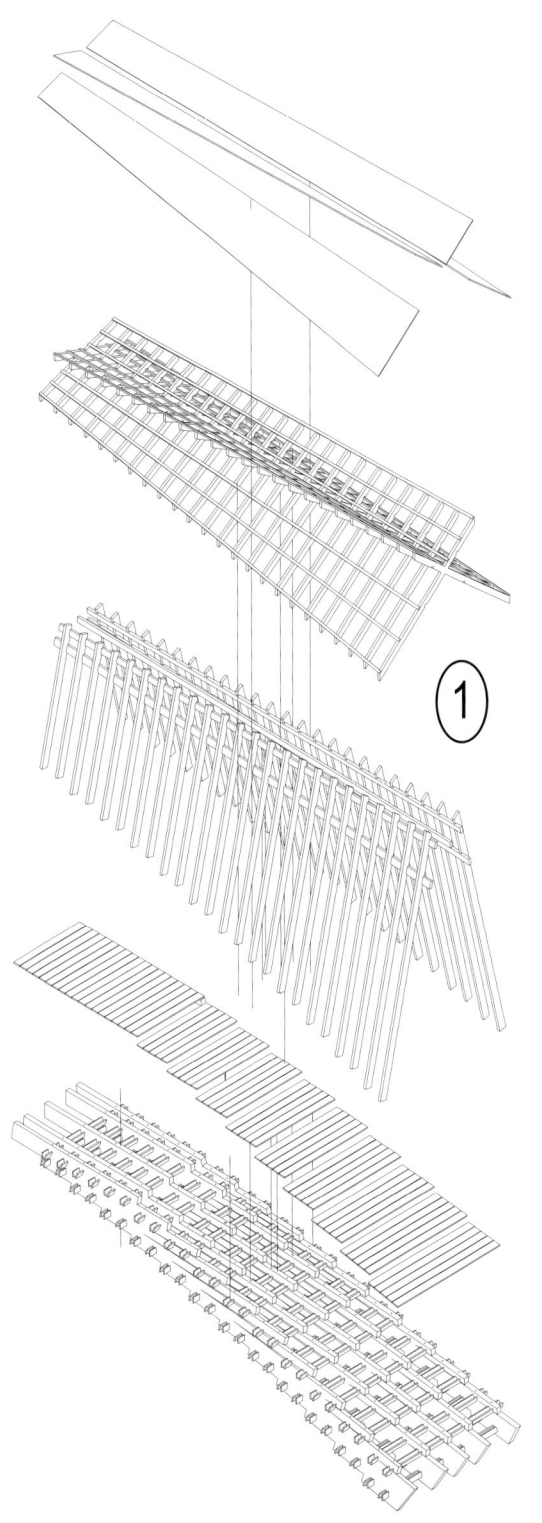

1. Do you think the central beam (Type B) is necessary? Can we assemble one full span and measure its deflection? This will be good anyway to test the construction process. If the beams are too heavy, we will need to work in-situ and joint sections directly on site—this will be more difficult;

2. Test joints do not fit tightly enough, more precision is required. We tested tolerances in model, loose joints create large deflections, and compromise strength of the entire bridge;

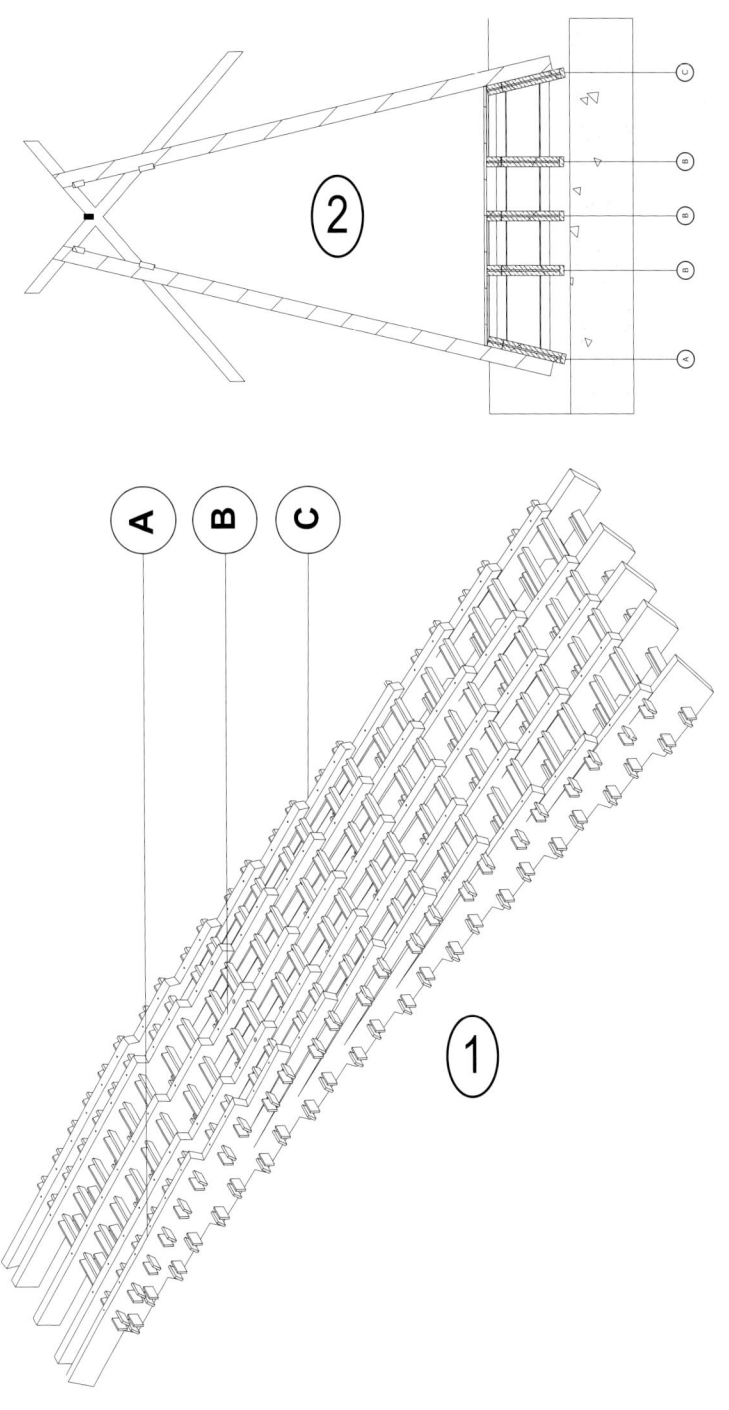

1. Use the jigs for the joints provided. The drawings are for reference only—students will help to translate the jig code for carpenters;

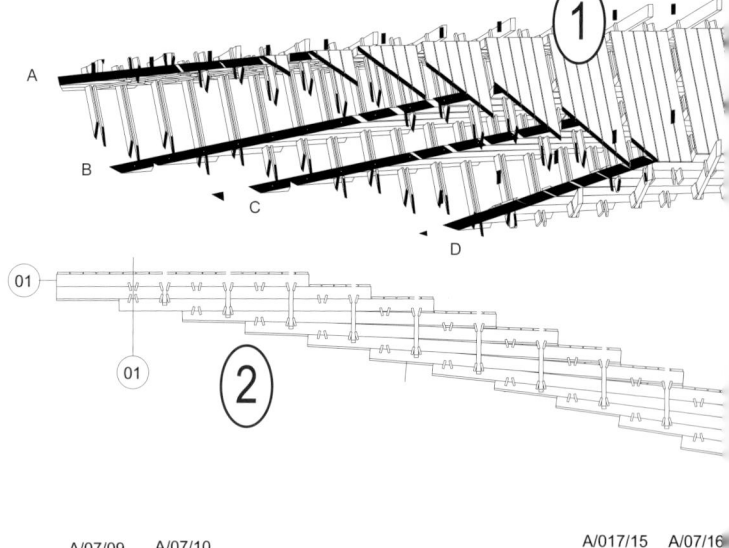

2\. Remember, the joints cut into the central beams are orthogonal but those on outer beams are composite angles. This tilting, in combination with the tapering of the structure, provides the lateral bracing;

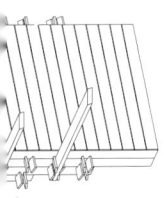

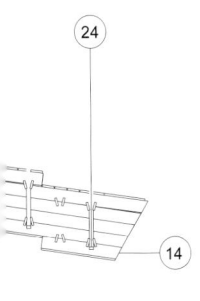

A/07/09	218 - L_34 / 73° 101° -- R _52 / 103° 72°
A/07/10	418 - L_32 / 91° 82° -- R _35 / 103° 72°
A/07/11	618 - L_35 / 105° 93° -- R _52 / 72° 103°
A/07/12	1018 - L_34 / 108° 93° -- R _35 / 72° 103°
A/07/15	1418 - L_34 / 73° 101° -- R _48 / 103° 72°
A/07/16	2618 - L_34 / 73° 101° -- R _52 / 78° 101°
A/07/17	3018 - L_34 / 73° 101° -- R _48 / 103° 72°
A/07/18	3418 - L_79 / 102° 101° -- R _52 / 103° 72°

1. Sketch for information only! —Song Shu to provide shop drawings. Please undertake as little intervention to the existing foundations as possible;

2. It will be simpler to change the formwork to brick, which will then become the new face of retaining walls. The timber work is too difficult for the contractor;

3. Youai—failure of the original footings was possibly due to a missing land drain to the rear of the retaining structures. Can you ensure Song Shu fits a drainage channel before he back fills the retaining work?

4. Important! The bridge should "float" to allow for expansion and contraction of the wood. Do not bolt the beams to the reinforced footings;

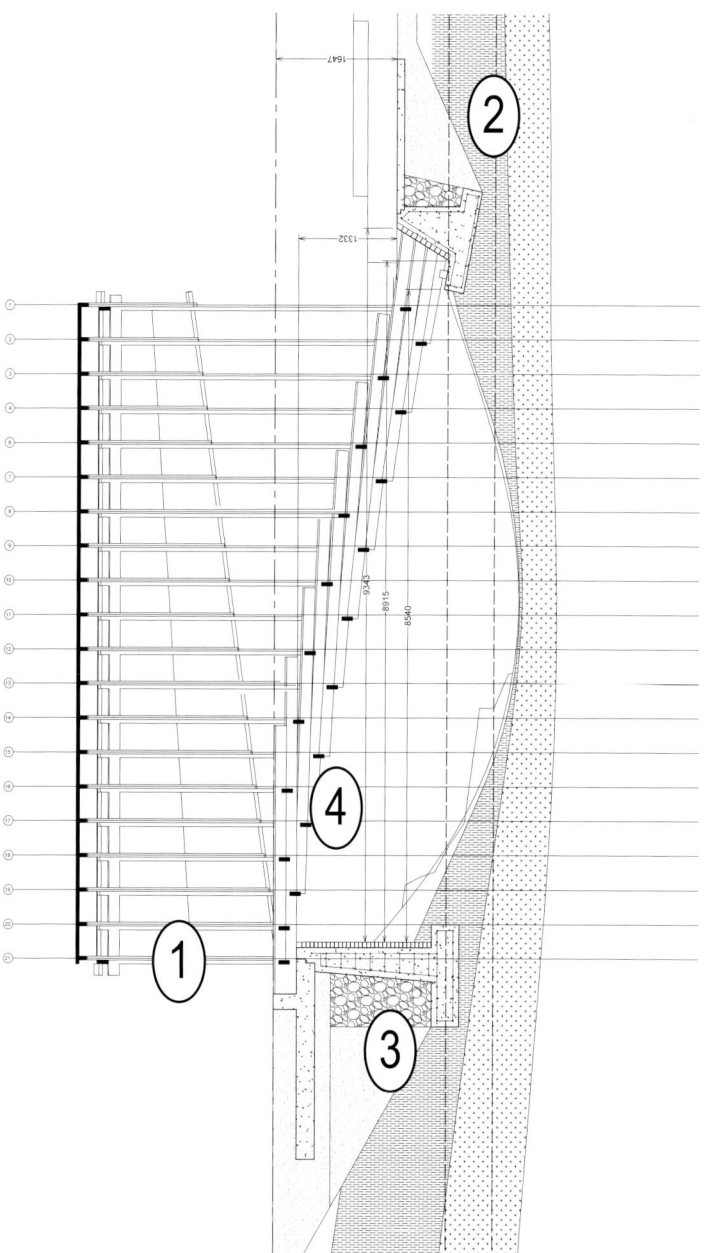

1. Once beams are installed and braced, we will need to install the horizontal wedges quickly. If the structure gets wet and expands, the joints may become too difficult to fit;

2. Start from west bank and clamp A1/A5, B1-B5 and C1/C5 together temporarily using the straps and rods—only install wedges once fully aligned;

3. Do not remove rods and straps until all elements in the same beam are wedged and braced. Students can help with alignment on bank but should not fit the wedges themselves;

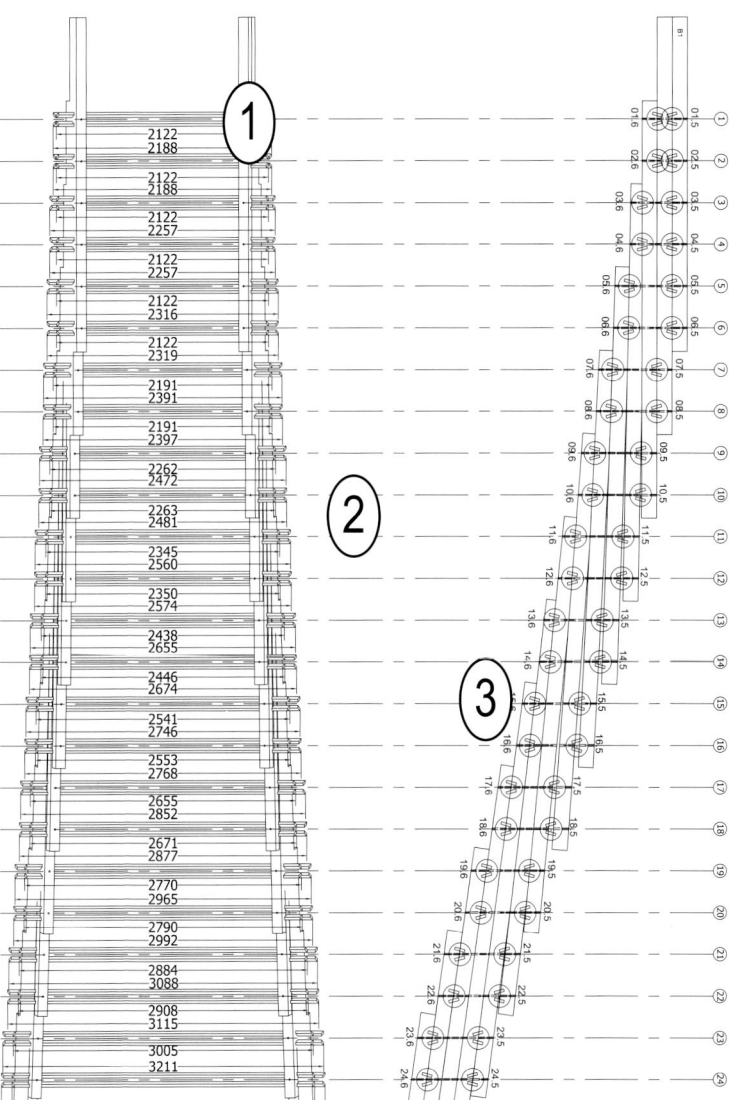

1 No nails required in the upper frame—it follows the same principle as the beams. The straightening of the beam as it settles will "lock" the upper joints—the shallow camber created is within tolerance!

2 No jig provided for the upper structure, but joints are simpler—students will mark out and the carpenters will make the cuts. The joints at the foot of each column are crucial! Let's have two teams—one marking and one checking;

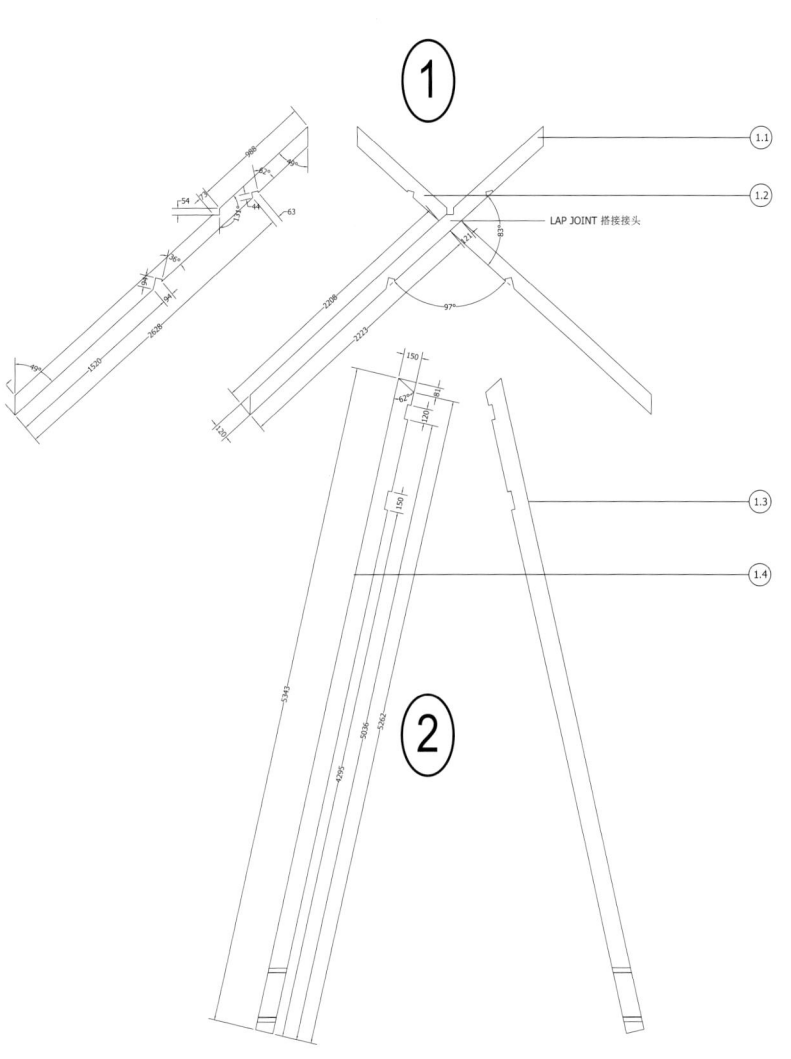

1   Youai! The tapering of each section within the beam is intentional—do not correct. They are necessary in order for the bridge to step from one bank to the other. If the joints require further stiffening, the design allows for additional wedges to be fitted following installation;

FRONT 面前
BACK 背部
CENTERS 中心
3201

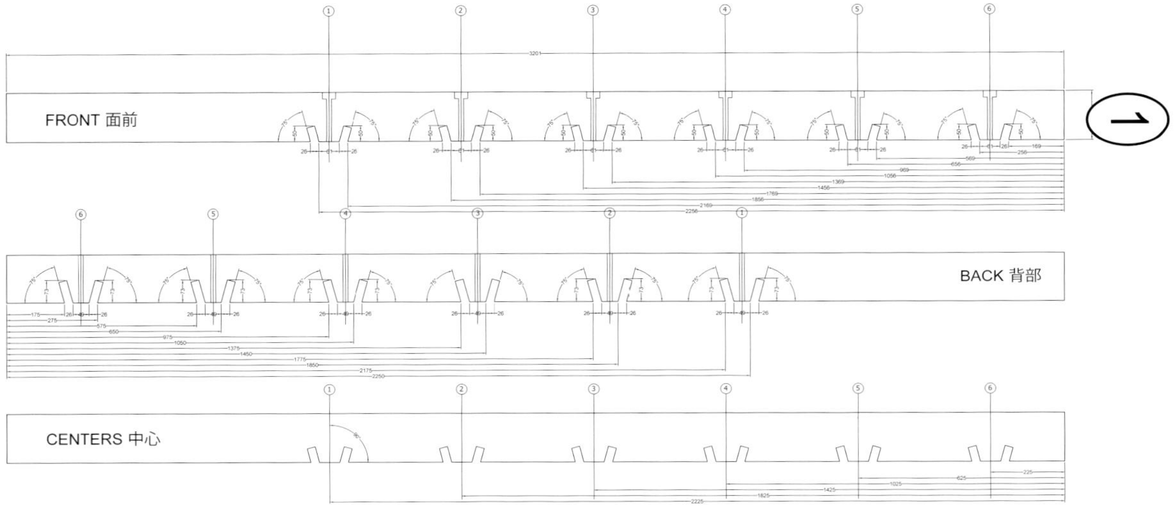

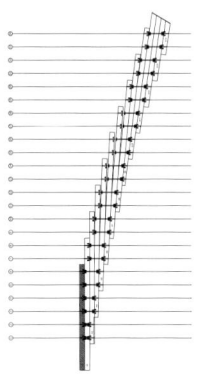

A1

1. Revision. Strength of timber samples provided does not match tables. Selfweight of structure needs to be reduced in order to prevent a noticeable beam deflection. We will need to reduce number of columns by 50% but maintain existing number of splines;

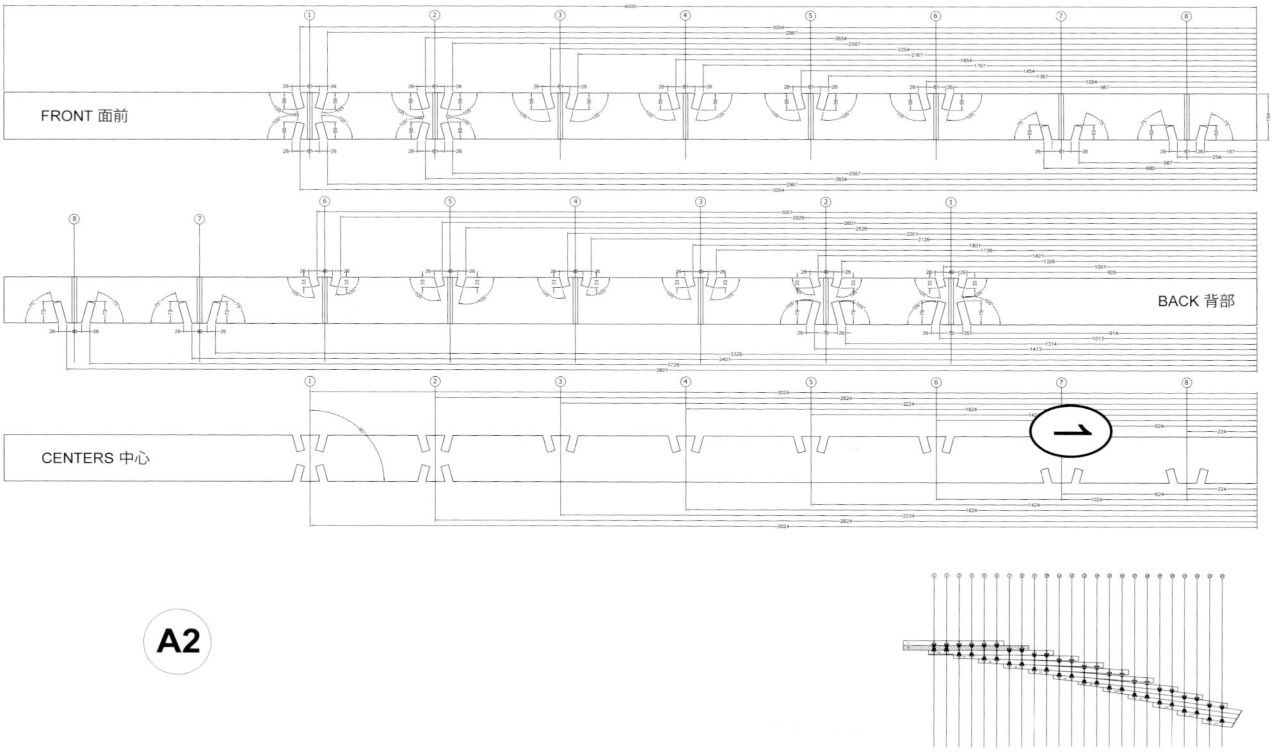

FRONT 面前

BACK 背部

CENTERS 中心

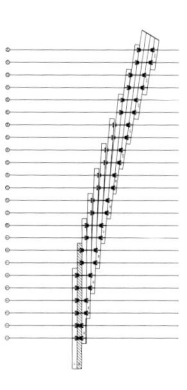

A2

1   Wedged Stop Bladed Scarf:
    Stop bladed scarf joints are used to create longer beams out of shorter elements. Good quality structural timber is in relatively short supply in the village.

2   Typical Mortise and Tenon details at columns: In general, there is an extensive use of wedges and bamboo pins (nails) to lock each joint in place. Typically, the primary structural beams are not sawn and planed as the timber section size is too small—instead the bole is shaped and leveled by hand, with an adze. As a result, these elements retain much of their natural character, however, great skill is required in their fashioning.

3   Housed Blind Dovetail: Glue is not used in traditional joinery (climate?) all joints rely solely on their mechanical strength to function—the dovetail is well used even if not always apparent.

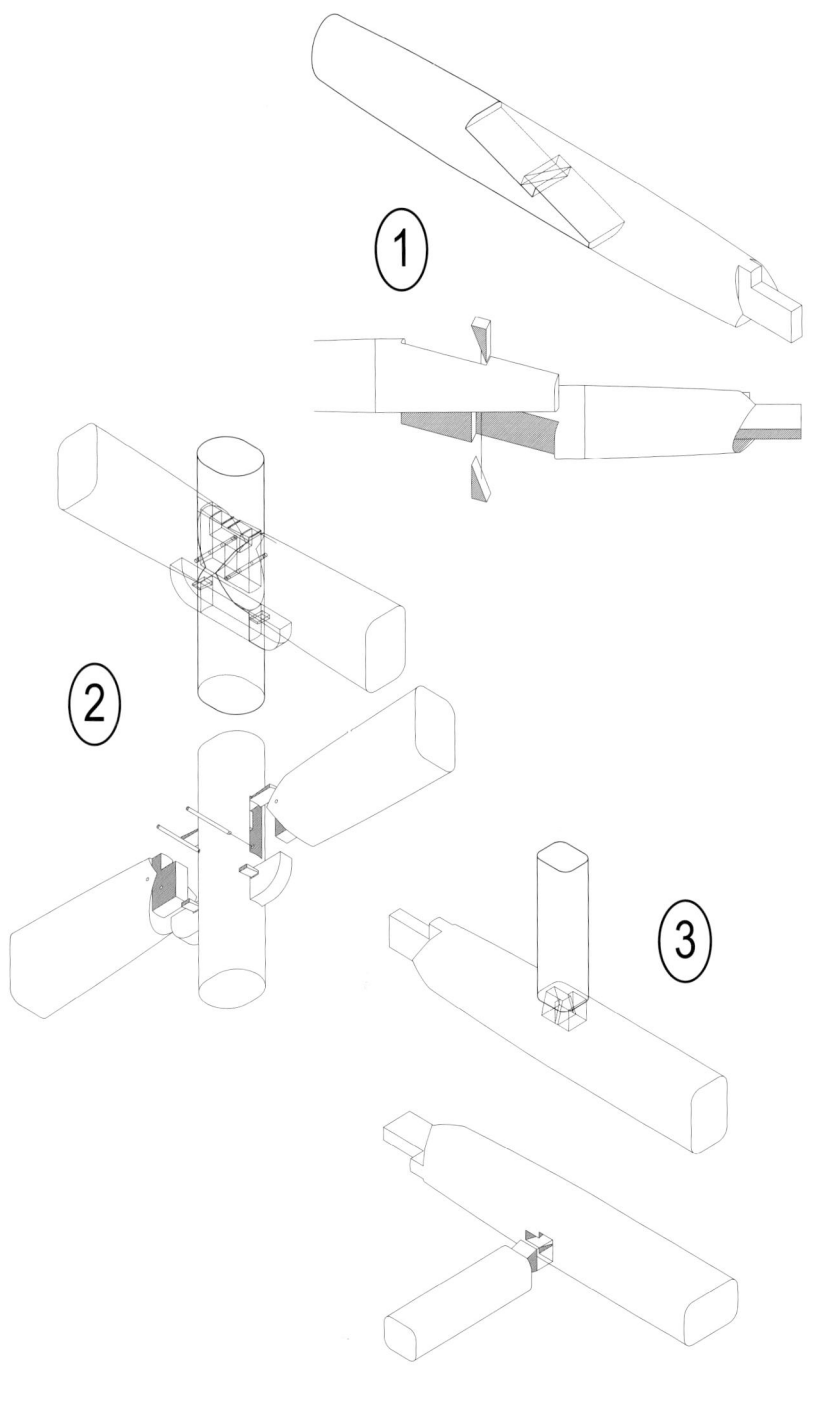

1   Wedged and Braced Dovetail Spline: The material intelligence borrowed from the joinery of Peitian is reinterpreted in the bridge via a digital process which reduces the complexity and the number of steps required to complete each joint while testing the potentials to expand the possibilities and responsiveness of the overall system;

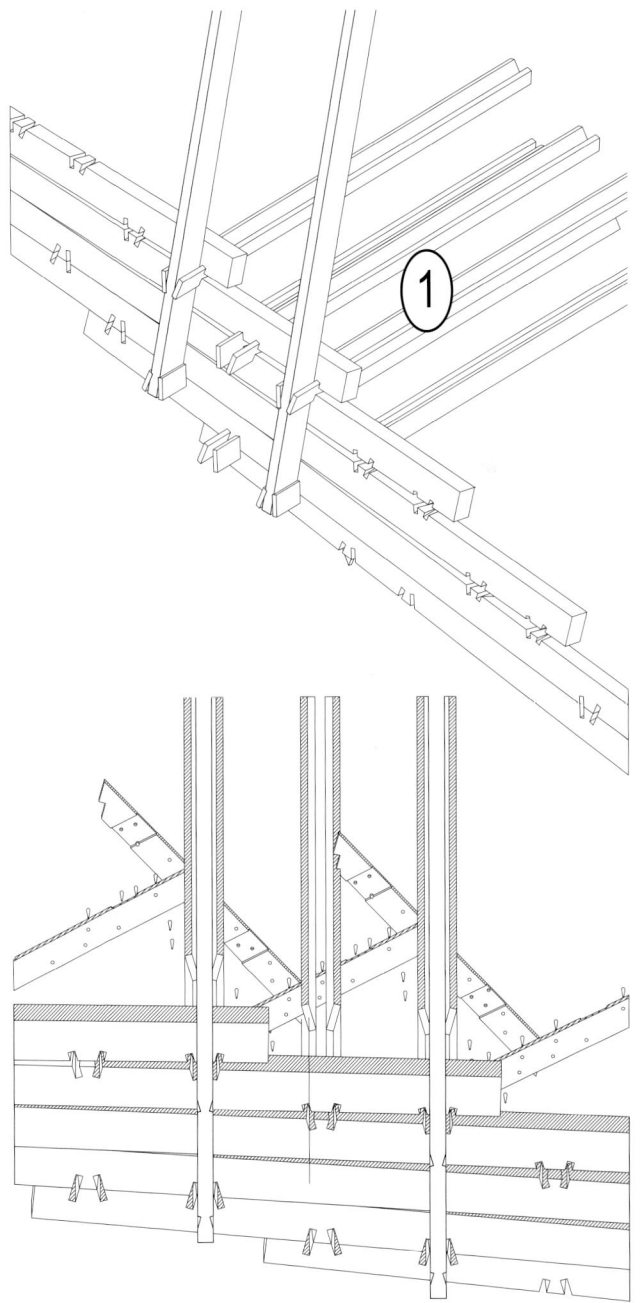

Village carpenters assemble the primary elements using traditional tools. A family enterprise spanning three generations is represented. Skills and techniques are passed down through the building process.

While village carpenters locate and position individual beams, students begin "lacing" them together using wedges and splines—carefully ordering and sequencing the construction.

Nearing completion, the evolving structure is inspected by local government officials. The construction site becomes a platform for the discussion of local heritage, tourism, and craft.

EXAMPLE 6: SUN ROOM

1. Nomenclature; A denotes a radial member while AB denotes tangential bracing;

2. Tangential bracing runs counterclockwise from A27 to A18 from Toe Plate to Node and clockwise from A2 to A27 and A18 to A5 from Node to Toe Plate;

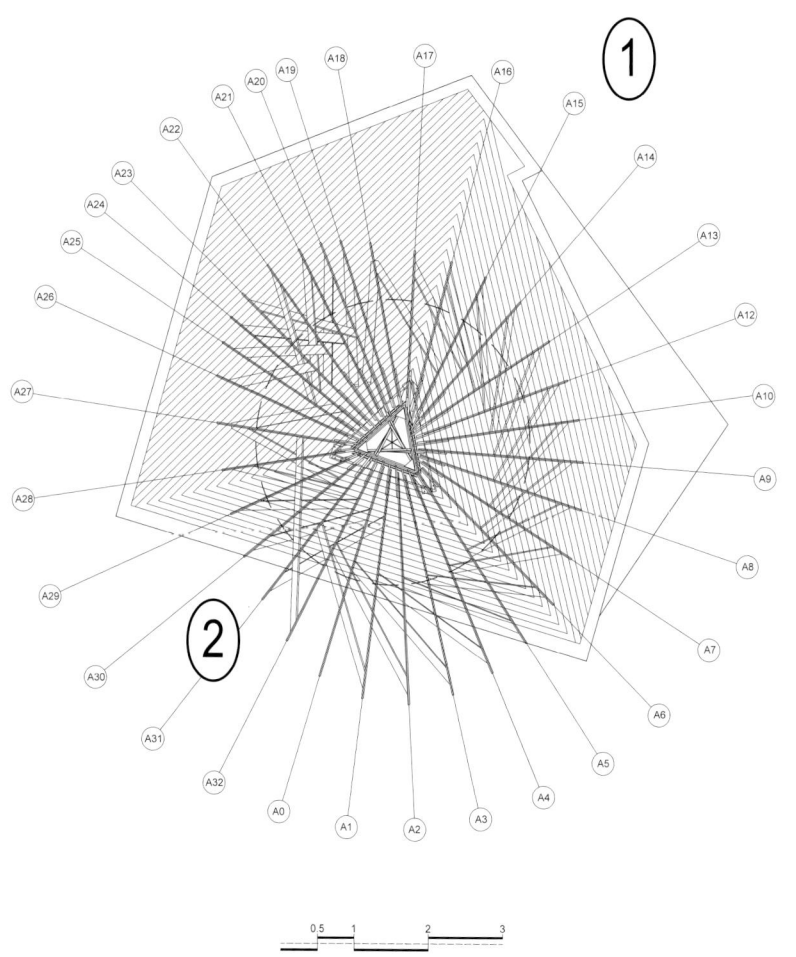

1. The wooden frame is essentially a machine for producing the skin! The steel rings are made on site, they do not have to match the model—instead we should work with the as-built condition.
The goal is a continuous curve with no kinks;

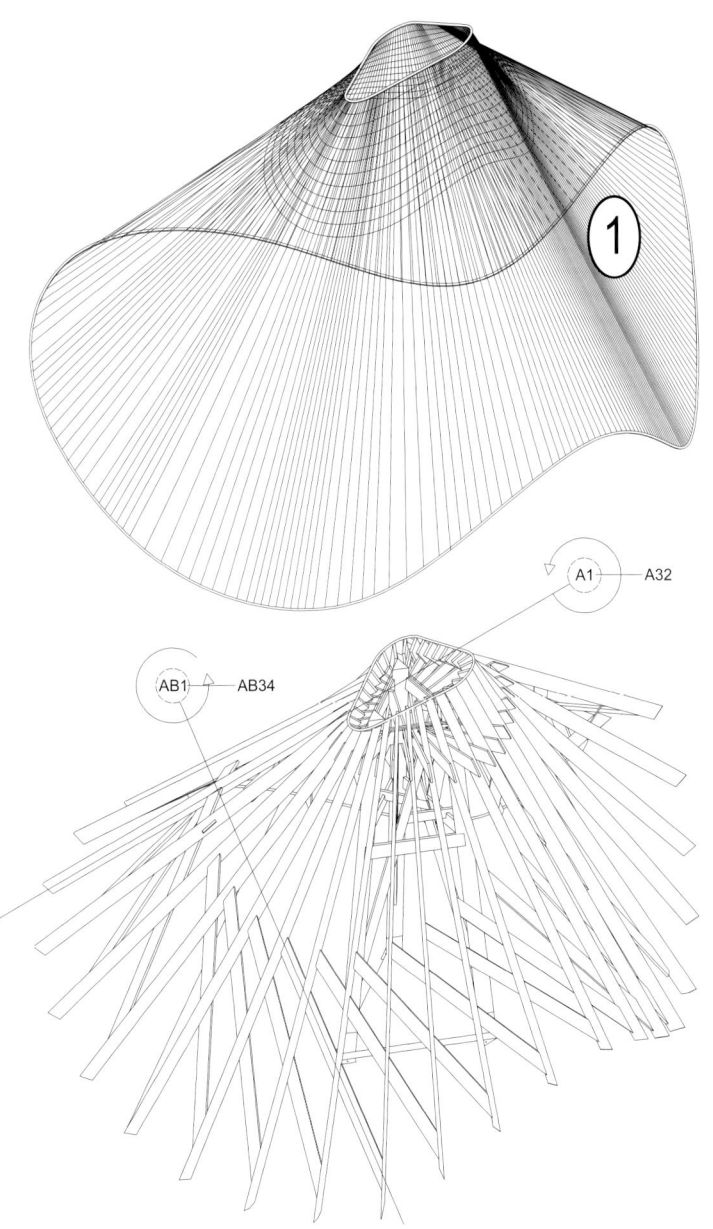

1   The central column is both scaffolding and formwork for the central node—this is the first element to be constructed on site;

2   The inner face of the node is angled to match the central column and will self level;

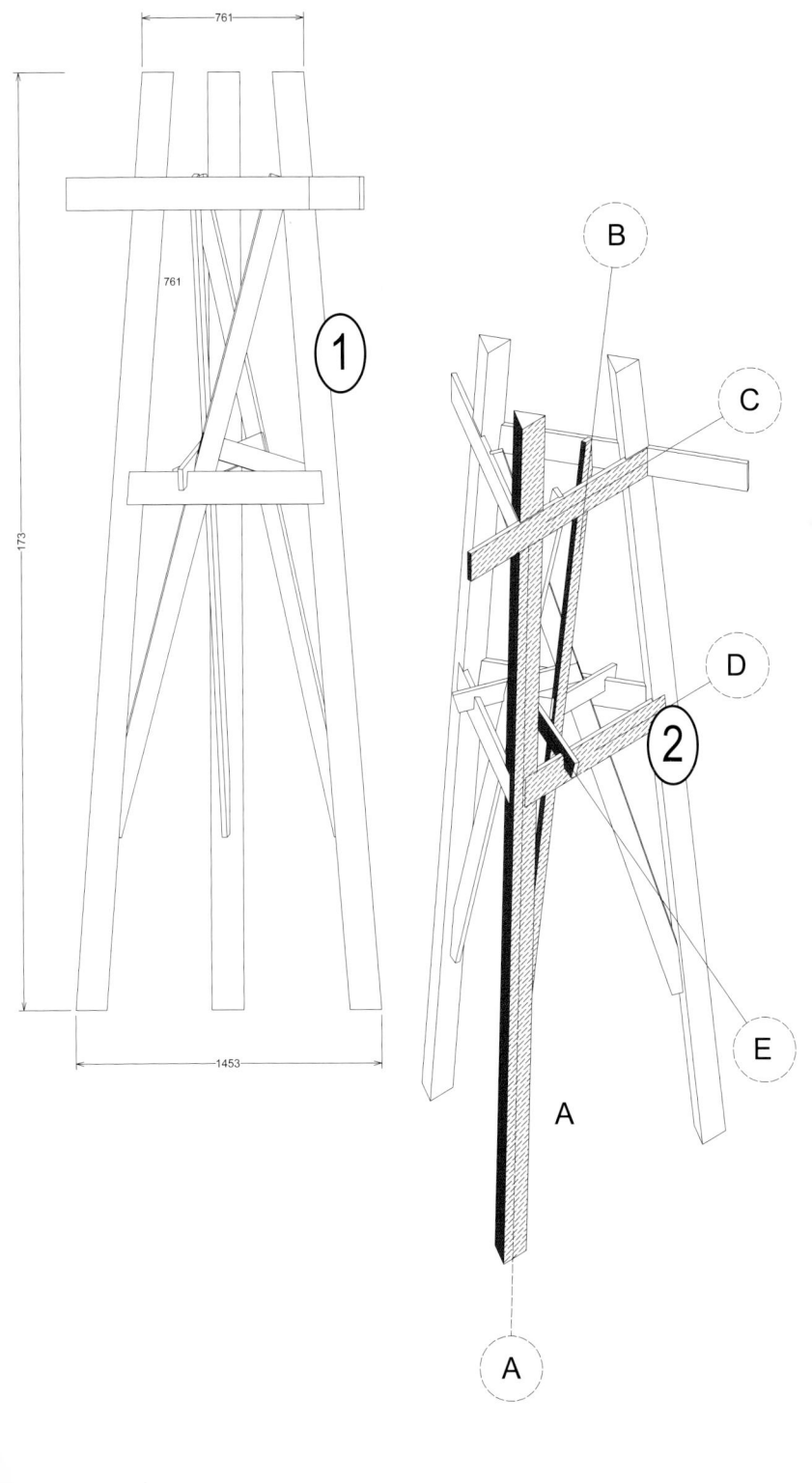

1	The column should not require mechanical fasteners if the joints are accurate;

2	The node acts as a strap and will bind together the structure—there are just five components in total that repeat a total of three times;

3	The production of each element follows the same marking and ordering principle as the bridge, we are short on time so it would be best if we can prefabricate these before students arrive. Students can carry elements to site and assemble there;

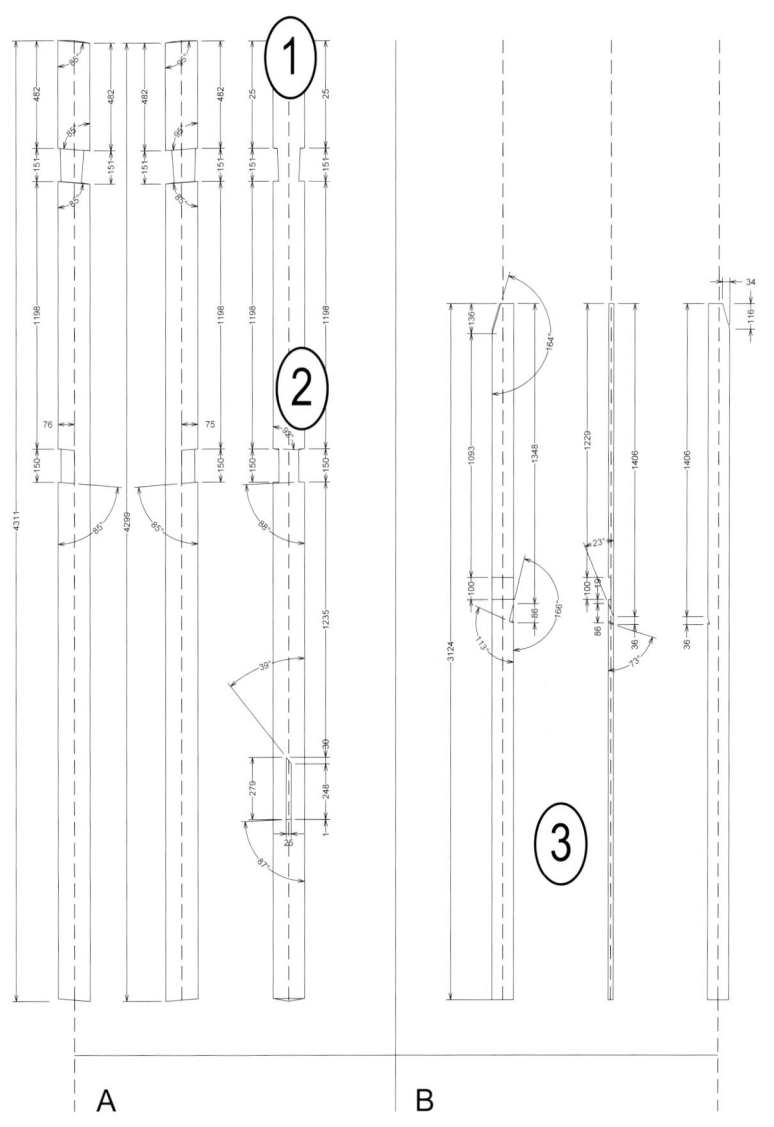

1   The node is the first thing to assemble on site. It will determine the position and angle of all the radial elements. Make sure to double check the assembly against the model to correct the node once it is assembled and installed on the central column;

2   Can you buy a large suitcase, measure it, and ensure all components of the node fit inside? We will machine in the lab at HKU and bring with us to site. If we need to redesign the node that's okay;

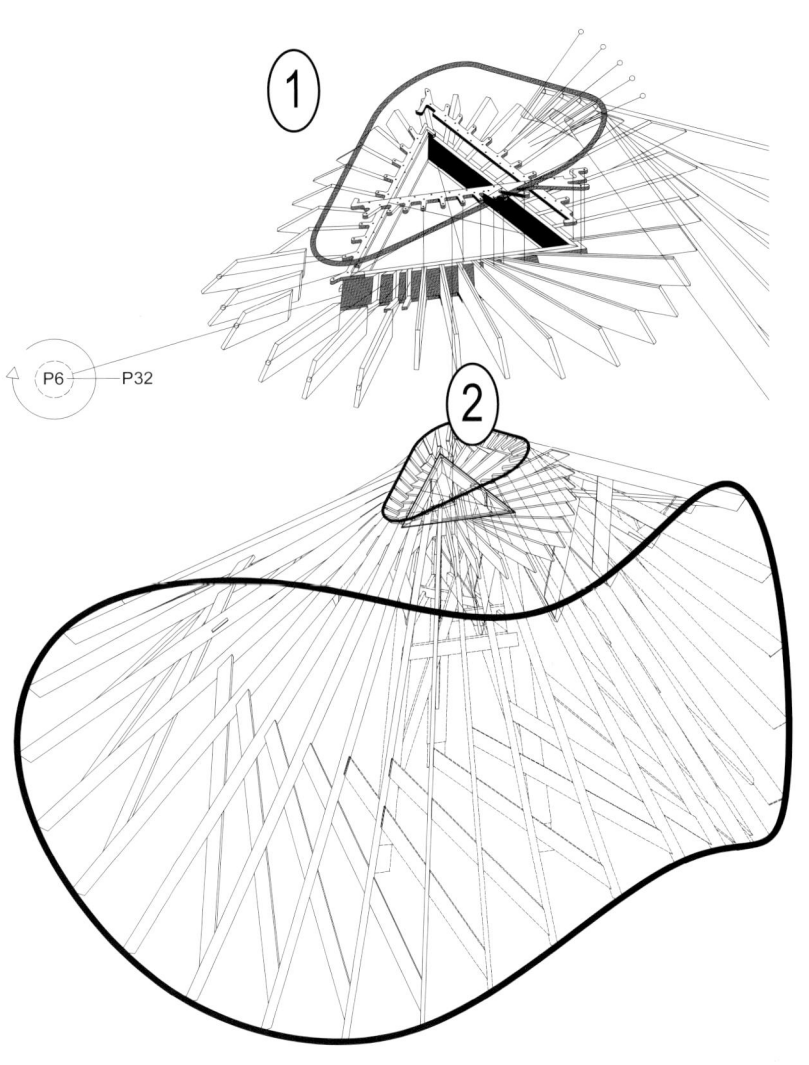

1   The diameter of the metal ring must be large enough so that the bamboo cane can wrap it. The material is brittle and it will snap if the radius is too small;

2   Bundle smaller thinner sections of steel rod to form the rings—the large diameter steel sections will be too difficult to bend in situ;

3   Pocket cuts on the radial members will make assembly on site possible, while not structural they provide element registration allowing for rapid construction;

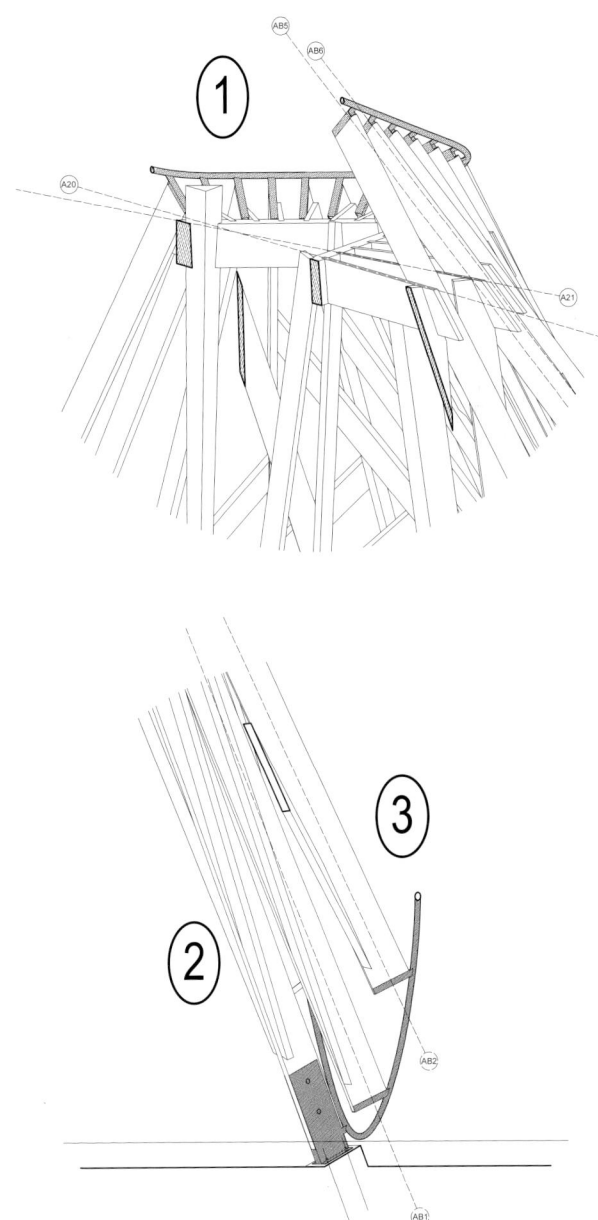

A model to be used on site that demonstrates the weaving strategy. The pattern map is informed by the bending radius and torsional limits of the bamboo cane.

The center of the Sun Room—a tool and a building component, prefabricated at the University of Hong Kong, which allows for the accurate positioning of the radial structural elements.

Anchoring and shaping the steel rings of the loom in situ.

A wooden beam locks the framing elements in place prior to the shaping and fitting of the pavilion's steel rings.

The last bamboo weaver in Petain shares his skills with new apprentices during tests.

The pavilion's form is determined by the landscape in which it is embedded. It is carefully designed to avoid obstructing the many protected viewsheds that cross the valley.

STRUCTURES OF CHANGE

Pinch came to fruition from a series of constraints that had to address a lack of funding, an economy of construction, and the fusion of various design responses into a single structure.

It is the first of a series of three small timber structures, Pinch-Sweep-Warp, that presents the potential for built experiments to actuate unique, yet unresolved site conditions in remote parts of China.

It does so by putting forward a flexible method of timber construction, informed by the work of the Spanish architect-engineer Felix Candela on linear geometry for the construction of curvilinear concrete shells. Specifically, it draws from his invention in rationalizing doubly curved surfaces, or hypars, into series of straight line generators for the making of timber formwork, made of straight elements only.

Building on Candela's work, the economy of the straight-line is once more tested as vehicle to ease constructional means and absorbing low-skilled labor, while supporting specific architectural strategies impacting both site and program in unexpected and imaginative ways.

Economy of the Straight Line

What was remarkable about Felix Candela is the spirit by which he was able to take thin shell concrete to a completely new level via the inventive constructional methods and despite the humble means and resources by which they were built in Mexico at the time.

It is mainly by his maverick approach toward live experimentation on construction sites, that he was able to

Left: Rough concrete shell structure of Los Manantiales restaurant by Felix Candela, Mexico City, 1958.

incrementally push the limits of what his structures could do both physically and spatially. His body of built work can be read as one continuous project that evolved bit by bit, while taking on greater risks as his designs progressed over time.

Unlike most of his predecessors, he was not even a structural engineer by trade, but an architect educated in Spain. It is only after immigrating to Mexico during the Spanish civil war that he entered the field of structure in a rather unorthodox way, by first becoming a building contractor.

He was an architect who became a self-learnt engineer by necessity of having to build his projects. Although initially reading numerous academic papers on thin shell structures to update himself on the topic, he quickly saw the limitations mathematics or formulas had on the potential shapes of shells. Instead, and unlike his peers he re-directed the development of his structural design and analysis through a hands-on process of construction, which turned him eventually into a master builder.

Through full-scale experiments, he started off first by copying simple shells he had read about and their complicated structural calculations and theories. Learning by doing at incremental sizes, his construction company could suddenly take on more and more ambitious projects, specializing in concrete-shell construction and sponsored at the time by Mexico's industrial revolution.

He became a great innovator because he was working very closely with the properties of the concrete material, which was easy and cheap to use then, while simultaneously inventing new practical and efficient ways of building shells. It is via novel formwork strategies for concrete casting that he was able to empirically advance the performance and forms of his projects; such as with the better known hyperbolic paraboloid or hypar. A lesson learnt is that how something is made empirically, through a process of trial and error, can easily

Right: Workers concreting the shell for the Bacardi Rum Factory designed by Felix Candela and built in Cuautitlan, Mexico in 1960.

outstrip one made by theory only, to greatly benefit the final design outcome of projects.

The double curvature of Candela's complex shells (hypars) brought additional strength to the performance of his concrete structures. Yet, the straight-line generators describing them, via rotating parallel lines, allowed him a direct and simple translation of uneven curvilinear geometry in built formwork, made of straight boards only. His methods strongly conveyed simplicity of construction.

Through Candela's use of straight-line building method, sophisticated shells, such as the Los Manantiales Restaurant or the Chapel Lomas de Cuernavaca, were realized with economy and ease. Although labor intensive, they could be achieved with low-skilled workers, affordable materials, and cheap work force in Mexico at the time. This was an ideal recipe for an emergent economy with a low cost labor force.

Fast forward half a century later to China, similar limited working conditions and resources are at play in the remote Chinese countryside where Pinch was constructed. This in turn made room for other types (than from the Mexican context) of unexpected design opportunities for the project to arise as it developed.

During our first visit in Shuanghe Village, Yunnan Province, several possible sites were initially presented to us by local officials. Yet, they were just empty and flattened lots, devoid of any physical characteristics to work with, which could have limited the built project to a freestanding object (as in most of Candela's built work), rendering it financially unaffordable.

The project responds to the government reconstruction effort after the 2012 earthquakes that ravaged parts of Yunnan, China. Mud and timber houses in villages were destroyed, leaving residents in temporary tents while the rebuilding effort was taking place.

Left: Villagers living in temporary tents while rebuilding their own houses after the 2012 earthquake devasted parts of Yunnan Province.

After the earthquake, wood was deemed unsafe, old, and dirty and was quickly substituted for the construction of new houses by more sanitized and generic building systems, such as concrete frames with brick infill covered with glazed tiles.

Prior to beginning work on this first community project, our intent was to change the negative perception of the timber material by reenacting its cultural relevance in these remote areas of China through more contemporary uses and inventive methods of building with the old material.

The funding for this small project was very modest and the budget was barely enough to subsidize a foundation. Its construction, as a result, had to be planned in two phases; structure first, enclosure and furniture second. In anticipation, we predicted that siting Pinch against an existing piece of infrastructure, like a wall, would save considerable material resources and construction costs, while also providing extra lateral resistance to the overall structure in an area prone to earthquakes.

Instead, the solution to a restricted budget was to make use of the existing pieces of the village's incomplete infrastructure, surrounded by the extreme landscape. In consideration, we proposed to work with the recently built public and memorial plaza at the center of the village, as it remained vacant and unresolved.

While onsite, we discovered a large height division in the form of a four meters high retaining wall preventing direct access from the village houses above to the leveled public square below and leaving it mostly unused. Not only did we intuit a potential structural advantage, we also thought we could potentially resolve the issue of connection to this newly built plaza.

In addition to tackling the lack of funding, our initial intuition was that siting Pinch in this very location could further trigger a series of architectural opportunities and social responses that will contribute to the village revival.

As of now, the choice of material was set and the site for the future project selected. Our brief was to provide a small community center including a library for children as a means of galvanizing community spirit, dented by the earthquake's destructions in the village.

However, our first design focus was less communal and more infrastructural; how to utilize the building to connect the road serving the village above with the large and often empty plaza below, and in doing so further revitalize both sides?

The roof became the primary means of bridging the four-meter level difference of the sheared site, while simultaneously housing the library below. In fact, Pinch was designed upside down; first the roof acting as new active ground and infrastructure, then ceiling and structure, progressively descending onto the ground of the plaza, while describing the space of the library below.

Its definition had to be agile in order to integrate coherently and seamlessly many programmatic components at once, operating at various scales: a bridge, a viewing platform, a seating and play area, a room, a bookshelf, and a door.

The final spatial demarcation of the roof is created by two overlapping and opposing movements: downwards and upwards. At the short end, one motion starts flush with the road above to give access and gently descends along the roof's outermost edge onto the level of the plaza. As a result, it produces a long and irregular opening bringing natural light into the program below. The other counter movement occurs along the roof's middle ridge, rising progressively from flat at one end into a high-pitched gable on the other side. This, in return releases a high ceiling room beneath to further support a hanging bookshelf. Its high pitched profile also echoes the extreme vigor of the mountainous landscape beyond.

The design of this highly pronounced and irregular roof surface required the creation of a relatively flexible and evolving building system, which had to be incrementally tested in order

to be fully realized. Initial material tests were also necessary to establish the adequate construction method, before finalizing the overall geometry of the project.

To arrest roof to ground, 17 trusses sectioning the roof's irregular surface transversally make for the main structural principle. They begin as a small doorframe and end as a large and high gable. How the first progresses to the last in a coherent sequence is mediated by trusses of changing spans and assemblies made only of linear and standard timber elements. Each one is anchored along the length of the existing retaining wall and onto the ground of the plaza.

The trusses' linear progression to describe doubly curved timber roofs similarly draws from the work of Felix Candela using a hyperbolic paraboloid for thin concrete shell construction, discussed previously. The ridge lines of each of the Pinch's trusses operate in a similar fashion. They each rotate slightly in succession, from horizontal to doubly inclined. The degree to which these linear changes occur had to be informed by the very properties of the timber material itself, requiring a series of full-scale mockups before concluding the design of the project.

At first, a full-scale trial of a typical truss was constructed in the local carpenter's workshop. It helped determine the singular material cross-section to be adopted for the entire structure, the truss's own resistance or performance vis-a-vis maximum span and height, and its composition into three sandwiched layers of criss-crossing timber boards, simply bolted at joints.

The boards for the decking, running in the opposite direction from the trusses, needed to twist and bend to some extent in order to adhere to the double curvature of the roof, while at the same time being sturdy enough in cross-section to support human occupation.

Another full-scale mock-up tested the torqueing capacity of the selected size boards in two directions based on the spacing

Left: The dividing retaining wall of the newly built memorial and public plaza was identified as opportune site for the project.

between each of the trusses and on the degree of geometrical change from ridge to ridge. At this stage, a back and forth process had to take place between the different material testing and the hypothetical amplitude of the geometry of the project until a proper calibration between both was estimated to be the right fit.

The final production of the 17 trusses was made on site. Each truss's triangular geometry was first drawn by hand on the surface of the plaza, serving as a full-scale blueprint on top of which the truss members were then directly cut, placed, adjusted, and pre-assembled flat. One by one, they were then flipped vertically and secured at their respective location at the top of the existing retaining wall.

Once the array of trusses was installed, the rest of the construction naturally and smoothly ran its course. The sequence of built trusses acted as templates to ease the rest of the construction with its underlying geometry acting as the scaffold for the project.

Cross-bracing elements, sheets of aluminum for waterproofing, battens for the final decking, and railing completed the first phase of the project. Besides the added structural strength given by the doubly curved roof each building element, within the constructional hierarchy, contributed as well to the overall performance of the structural composite.

While pursuing extra funds to conclude the project, the raw structure was quickly adopted by the village's community, first as playground, slide, seating area, and bridge. Over a year later, the second phase focused on the completion of the library under the structure. Aside from rudimentary furniture for reading gatherings, translucent polycarbonate doors serving as both window and enclosure, its main feature was a hanging bookshelf; a natural extension of the roof's tectonics.

Left: Carpenters assembling the trusses flat on site, guided by the geometry of our construction drawings directly drawn full-scale by them on the plaza's pavement.

If the impression of the structure on the outside is one of rising forces toward the landscape, internally its spatial experience reads the opposite, mainly transmitted by the structure's ever-changing deep ceiling. The upside-down design of the structure concentrates on the definition of the roof as one single surface solving both the above and below. The ground slab is just flat. Yet, to further reinforce this sense of suspension on the interior some of the linear members of the trusses, activating the ceiling plane, were extended downwards to support the hanging bookshelf.

As one enters from a low and narrow door demarked by the first truss, and moves across the space toward the last wide and high-pitched truss, a peculiar sense of weight and lightness can be experienced from the changing scale of its interior; a sort of spatial expansion and tension when viewed from one end or a vertical and horizontal contraction when facing the other direction.

The moment Pinch became filled with books, the structure took on another dimension. Everything was solved in a single structure, demonstrating an economy of design where various programs at different scales coexisted as one integral unit. Doing this project brought to bear a new possible understanding of the environment in which we were invited to operate as architects. Yes, it is certainly poor but at the same time rich for a multifaceted experimentation that led to a surprising result that could have never been preconceived autonomously from first apprehending its physical context. At the end, a lack of funding can create innovative sites.

Although conceived as a temporary structure for the time of the earthquake reconstruction, Pinch still stands on the plaza. Since its completion, the villagers took over the project and even renamed it the "Open Book" because as they said, "it looks like one facing the powerful landscape and its main educational purpose has remained for reading activities." It is a testament to a simple appreciation of the project.

EXAMPLE 7:
PINCH

1. The retaining wall condition is approximated on drawings— I bet it's rough and not properly levelled. Let's make sure contractor surveys it before we arrive on site;

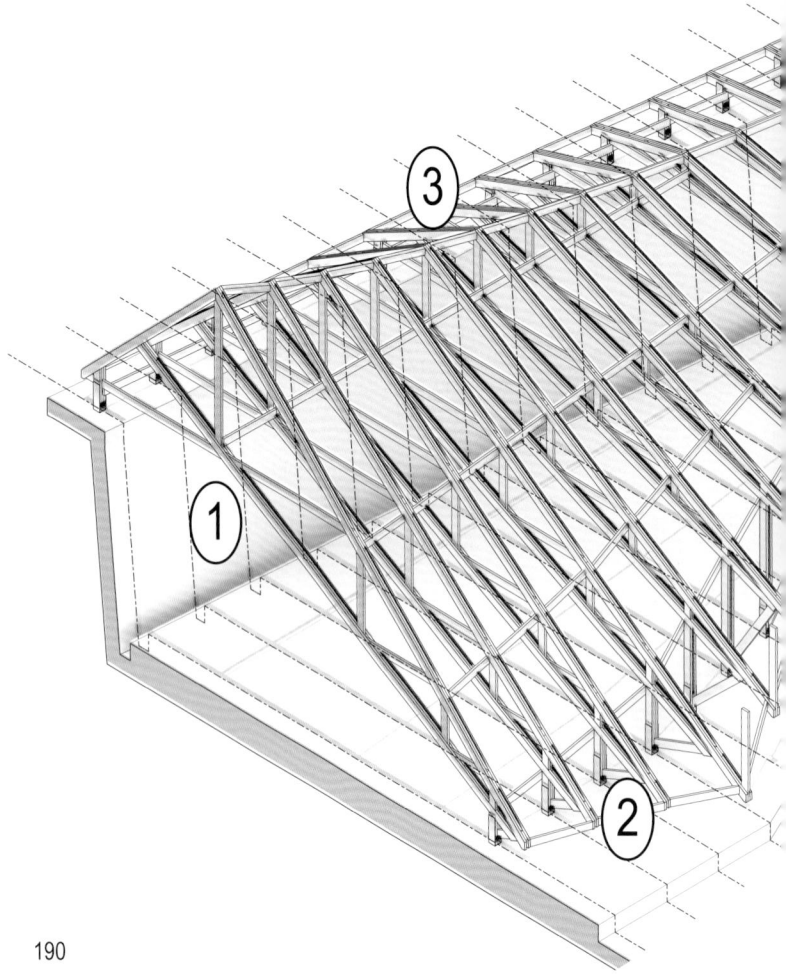

2   Local government is taking care of the concrete foundation: Did we send them the construction drawings yet?

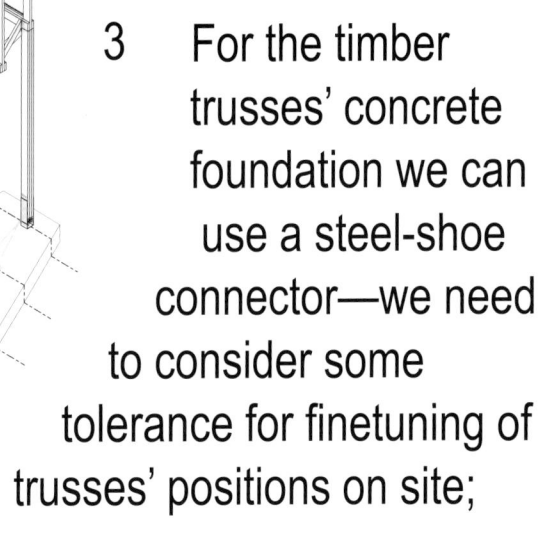

3   For the timber trusses' concrete foundation we can use a steel-shoe connector—we need to consider some tolerance for finetuning of trusses' positions on site;

1   The bookshelf hangs from the trusses—more like an extension than an addition! So need to adjust its geometry according to each truss;

2   Make sure the parapet stops earlier to allow circulation;

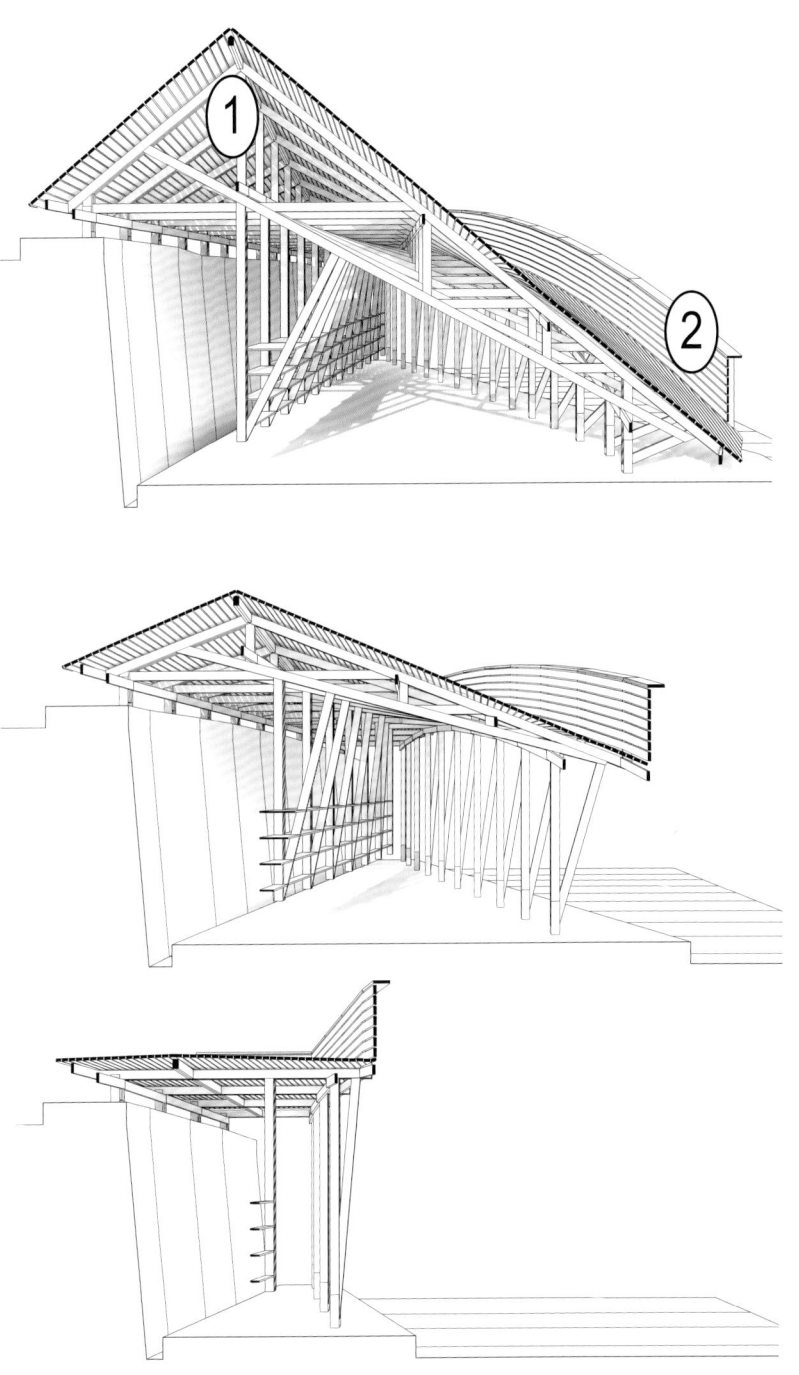

Top plan view of timber trusses

1   Shortest and lowest truss (T17) for main entrance;

2   Highest truss (T01) where bookshelf ends;

3   Longest truss (T04) where parapet ends for roof-plaza circulation;

4   All trusses (T01-T17) should overlap the retaining wall to prevent rain penetration;

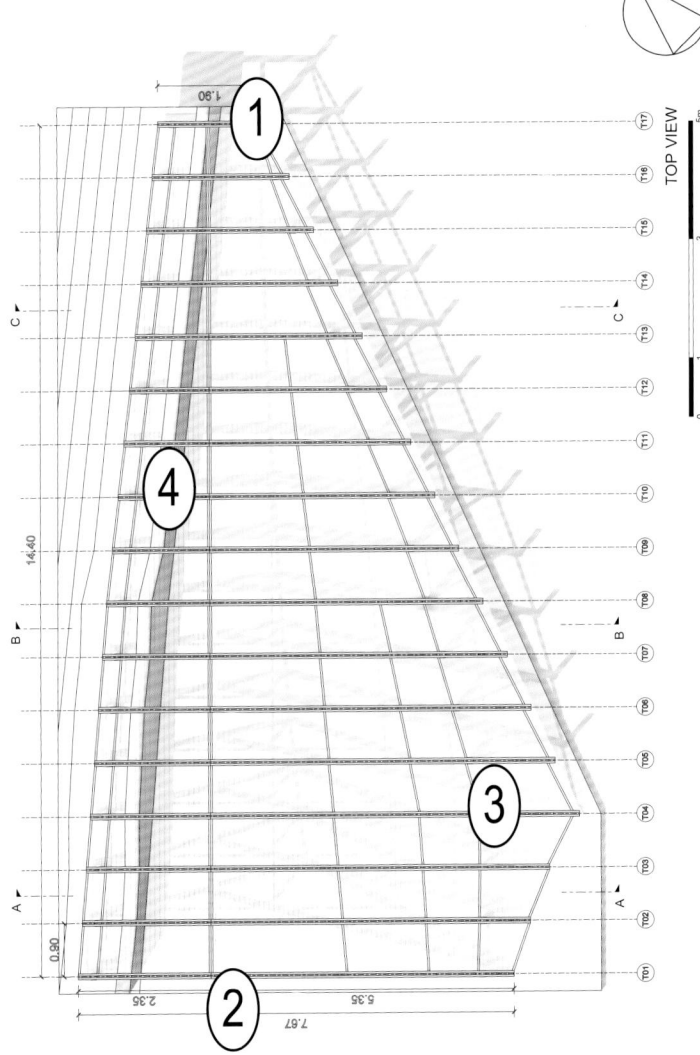

1. Catalog of trusses—double check dimension with carpenters when they will fabricate them on site;

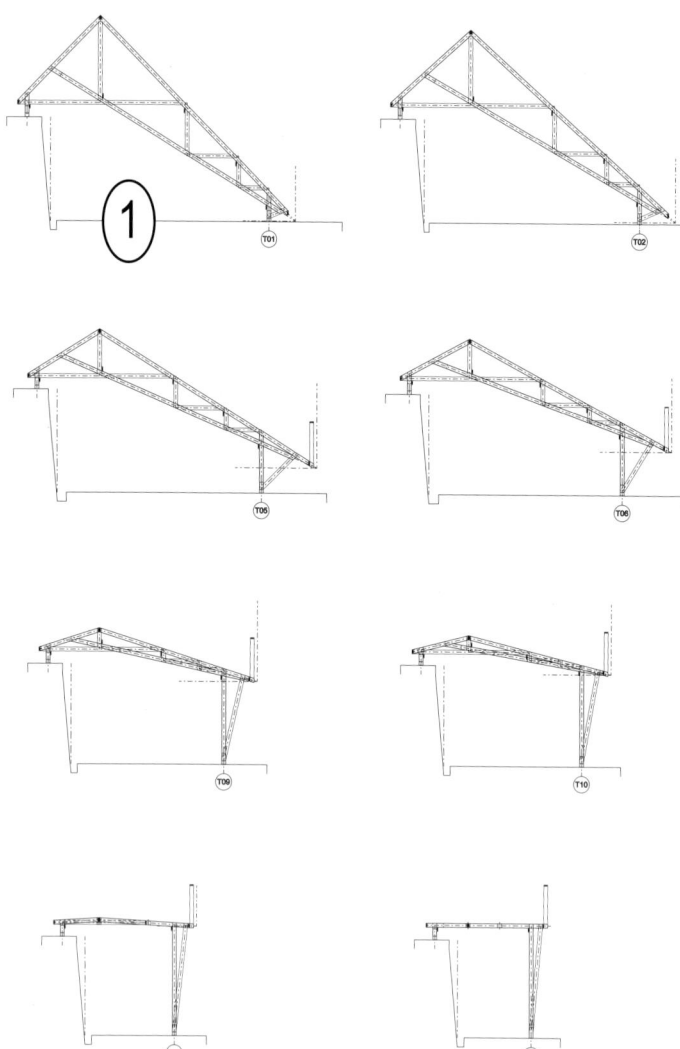

They can first draw dimension on ground and then assemble them;

2 Trusses are a three-layer sandwich: Double outside layers, single middle layers;

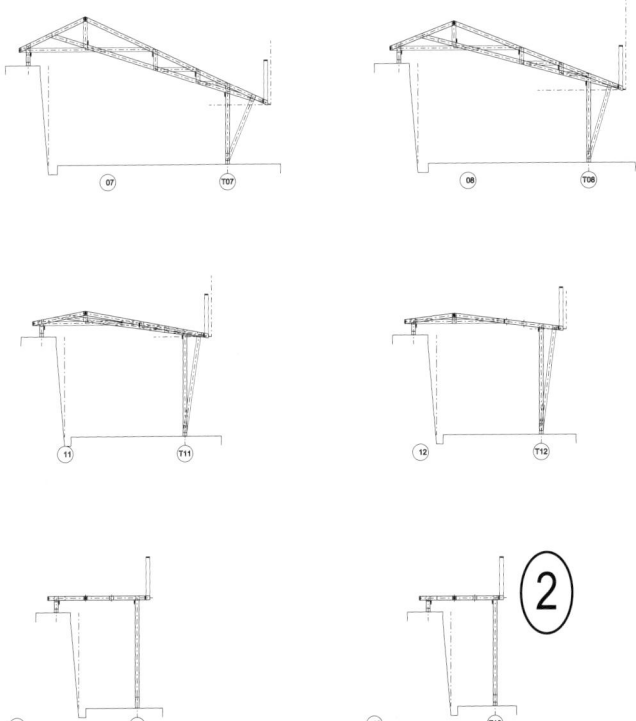

1. Parallel projection to assess geometrical progression of trusses—once checked, we can move onto construction drawings;

2. Progressive tilting of columns from vertical to diagonal;

3. Incremental lowering of roof slope to reach the ground of the plaza;

4. Gradual increase of heights of top ridge and depths of trusses;

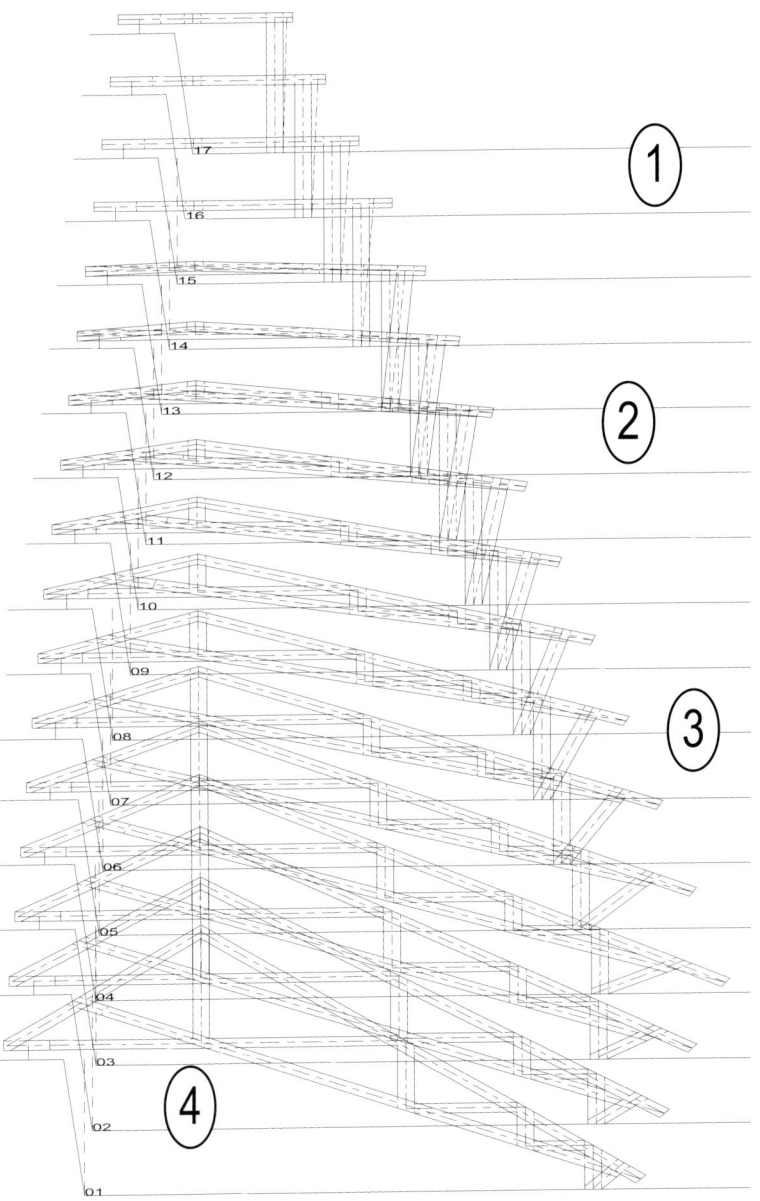

Instruction for assembling
a truss:

1   First carpenters should draw the main lines of each truss on the ground. These are the reference for the middle layer sandwiched between the outer layers;

2   Once principal lines have been drawn on the ground, position first layer of main truss beams;

T01

3.31
1.96
0.96
0.35
0.11
0.25
90.00°
2.32
3.37
1
45.00°
45.00°
7.54
5.63
2
2.05
1.23
3.24
0.65
1.23
45.00°
0.74
0.30
0.38
30.95°
66.76°
0.11
2.07
2.46
1.45
0.87
0.45
0.67
6.18
0.27
6.84
0.56

T04

2.57
1.39
0.85
0.30
0.11
0.21
1.45
110.77°
2.66
34.62°
34.62°
0.89
1.83
7.89
55.38°
4.72
0.58
1.29
3.20
0.36
1.41
25.89°
0.87
68.93°
1.18
0.11
1.85
2.23
1.51
1.06
1.12
0.60
6.05
0.27
6.65
1.69

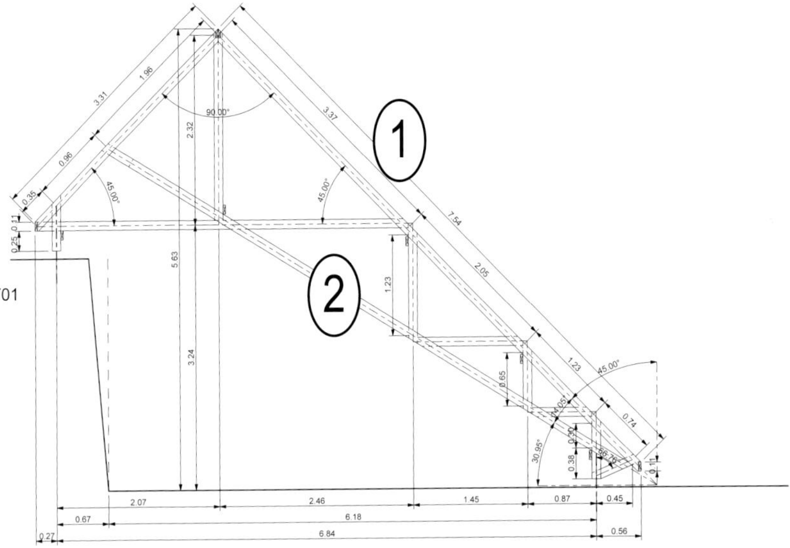

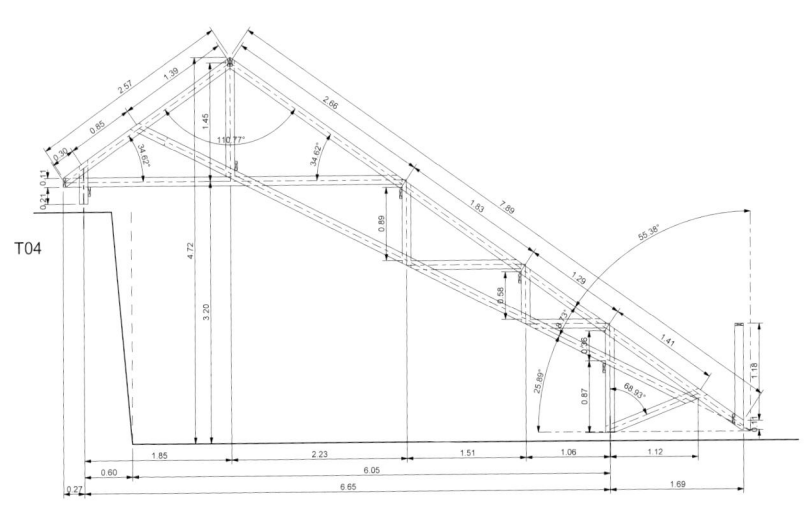

1   Once first layer of secondary beams is placed, position main beams (middle layer) and last layer of blue beams. Remember to trim all extra edges of middle layer past the secondary beams;

2   Don't forget to draw on plaza the groundline for proper orientation and reference of truss vis-à-vis ground;

T08

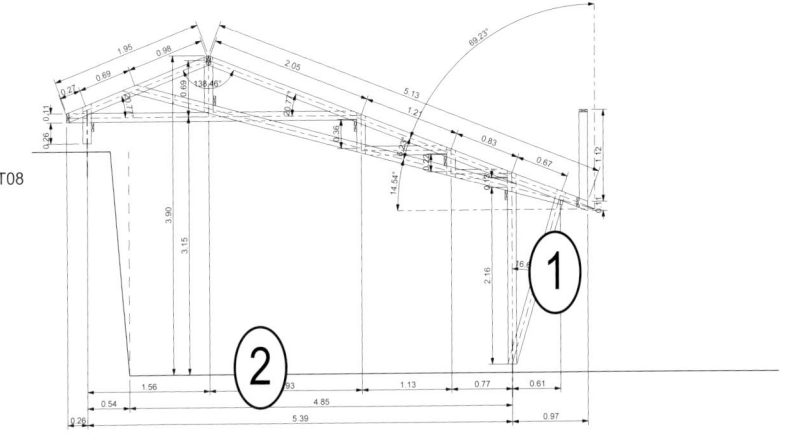

T12

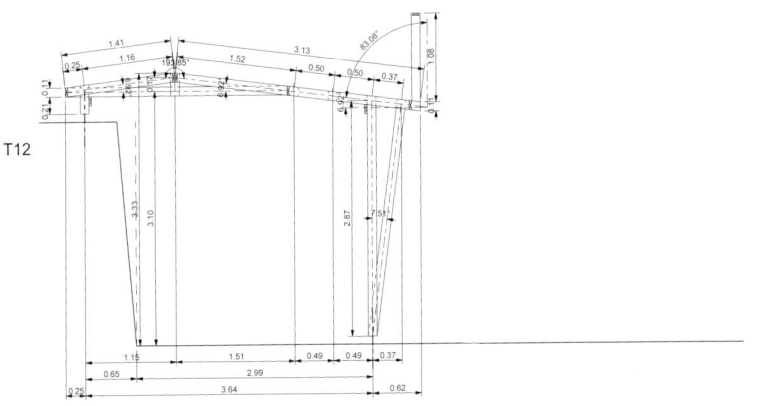

1. Follow principal truss lines for proper fitting of timber column into steel shoe;

2. Holes for steel shoe to be fixed to concrete foundation with epoxy bolts;

3. Locations of holes to drill through timber column once position secured, then use bolts to lock timber column inside steel shoe;

4. Leftover gap below timber gives tolerance for final adjustment of trusses on site;

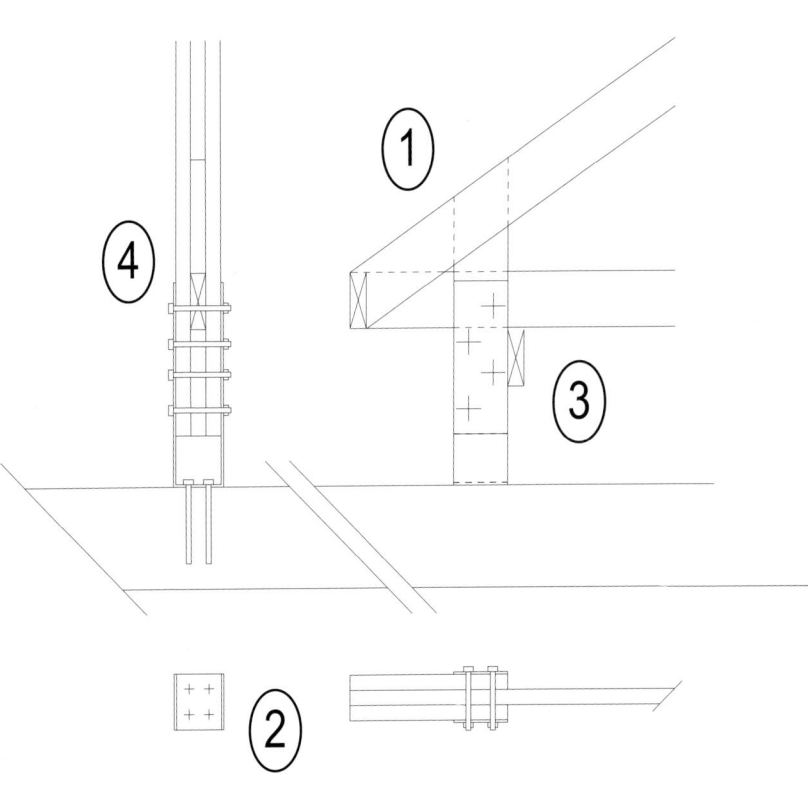

Piles of precut timber pieces for the flat assembly of each truss on site.

Once the truss elements are all correctly positioned flat on top of the full-scale drawing, the layers are securely bolted together for extra strength.

Right: Workers raising a truss into its vertical final position while taking advantage of the existing retaining wall for connection and stability.

The construction of the final decking begins at the top ridge. The last boards sticking out from the edge of the roof are then trimmed directly in situ.

Pinch in its rural and mountainous context.

EXAMPLE 8:
SWEEP

1. No need for a slab—a concrete ring is okay as foundation for the 12 trusses;

2. Trusses to be arranged radially and tangentially. IMPORTANT! They need to be connected to each other (both front and back) to stabilize the whole structure;

3. We want a double-curved surface from low to high—so even though beams are straight, they are rotated to one another;

4. Top decking: Straight boards, ruled-based, obviously perpendicular to beams;

5. Keep the parapets' materiality the same as the decking for visual consistency!

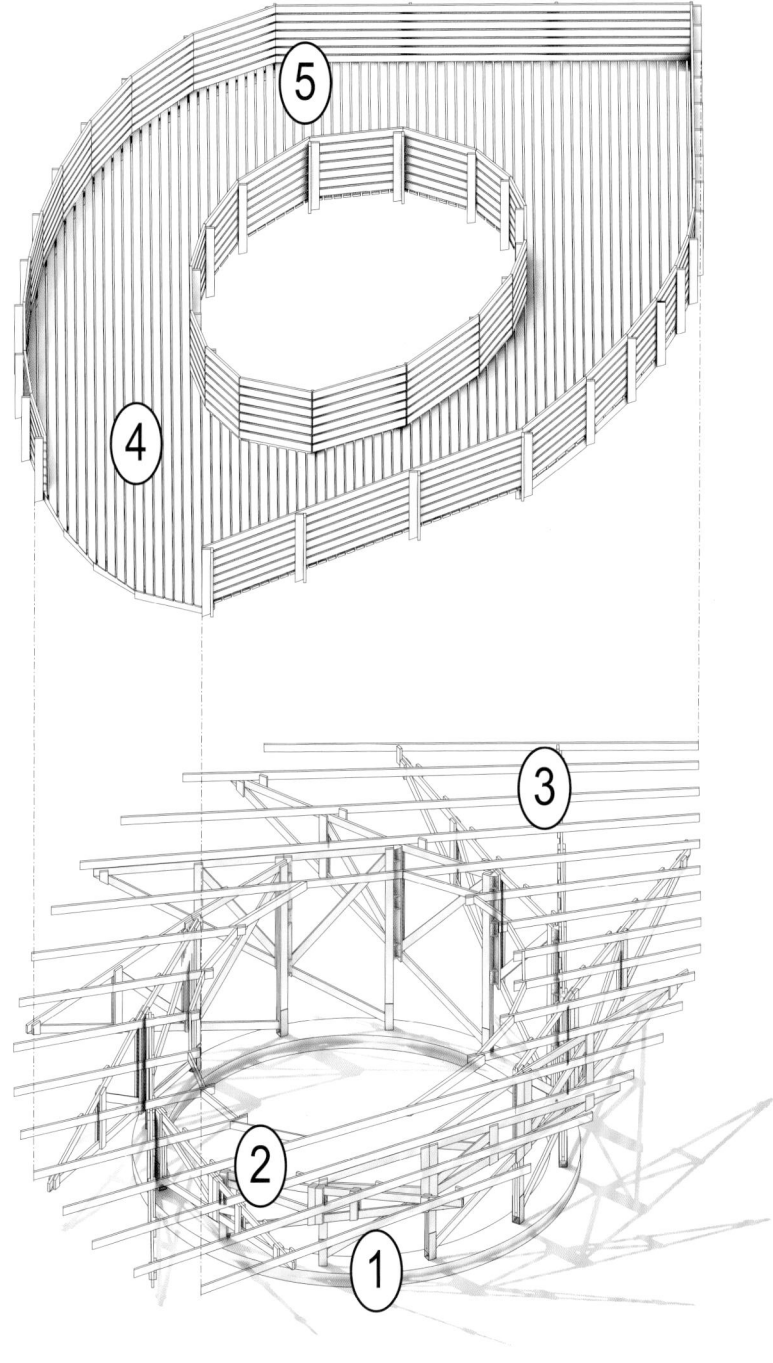

1   Use steel shoes to connect trusses to concrete ring foundation;

2   Use steel angles to connect the trusses to each other tangentially;

3   Attach ruled beams over the trusses with timber blocks;

4   Screw decking boards running in the opposite direction onto the straight beams and leave a 2 cm gap between them;

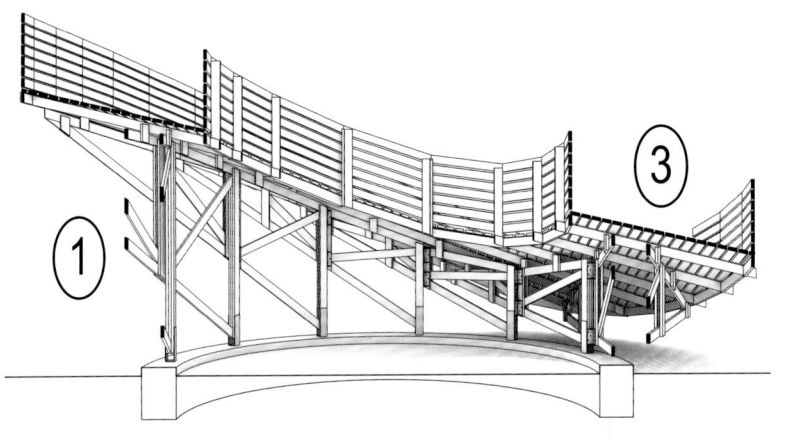

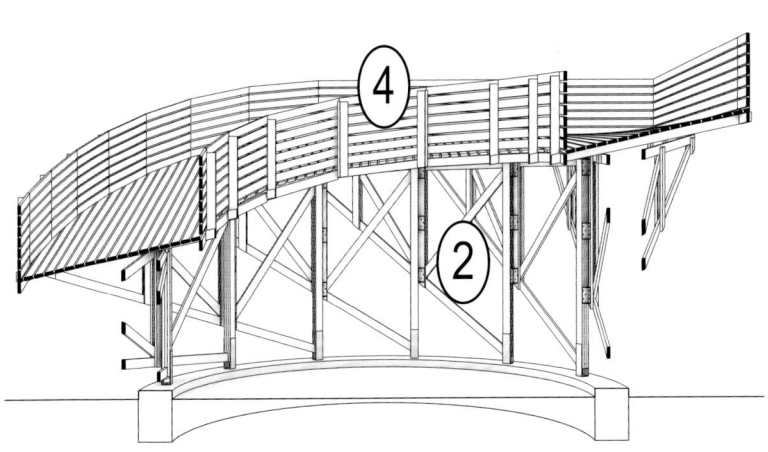

1   Place specified beam on top of its respective trusses;

2   Fasten beam on trusses with timber blocks;

3   Trim beam length to exact dimension;

4   Verify beam inclination with high and low dimensions;

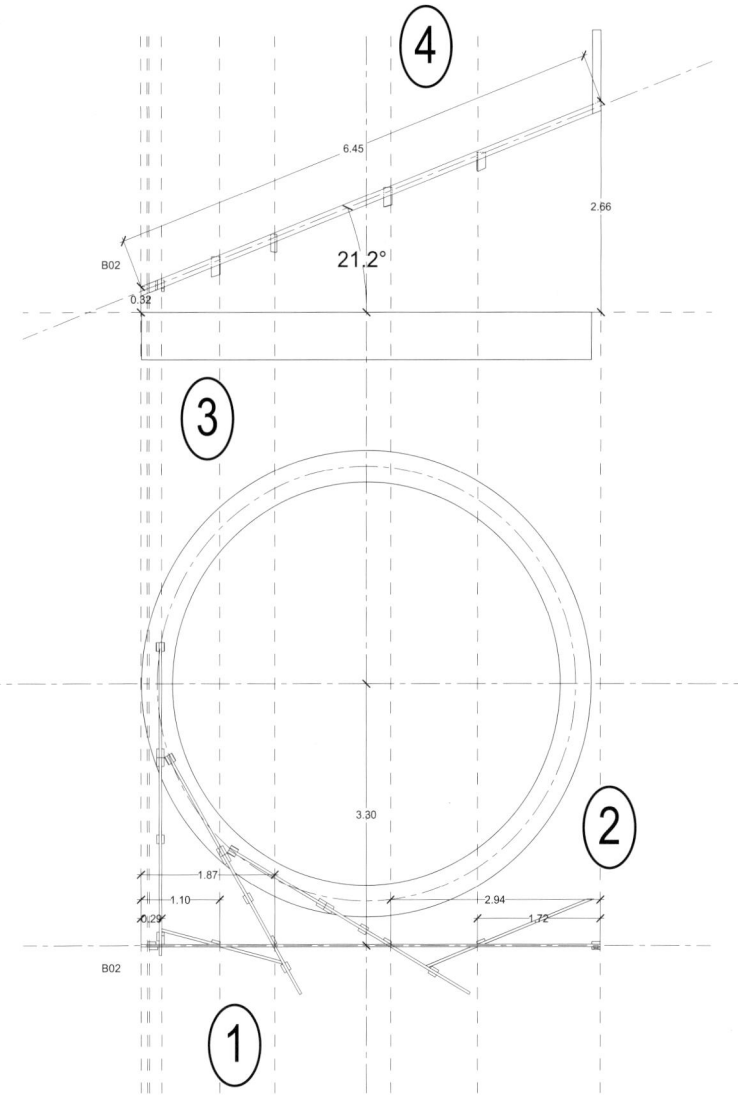

1. We should leave a gap between steel shoe and timber truss for final adjustment on site!

2. Predrill holes in steel for connection to ring foundation;

3. Predrill holes in steel for quick attachment through timber truss;

4. Use proper size bolts to guarantee strong joining of truss into steel shoe

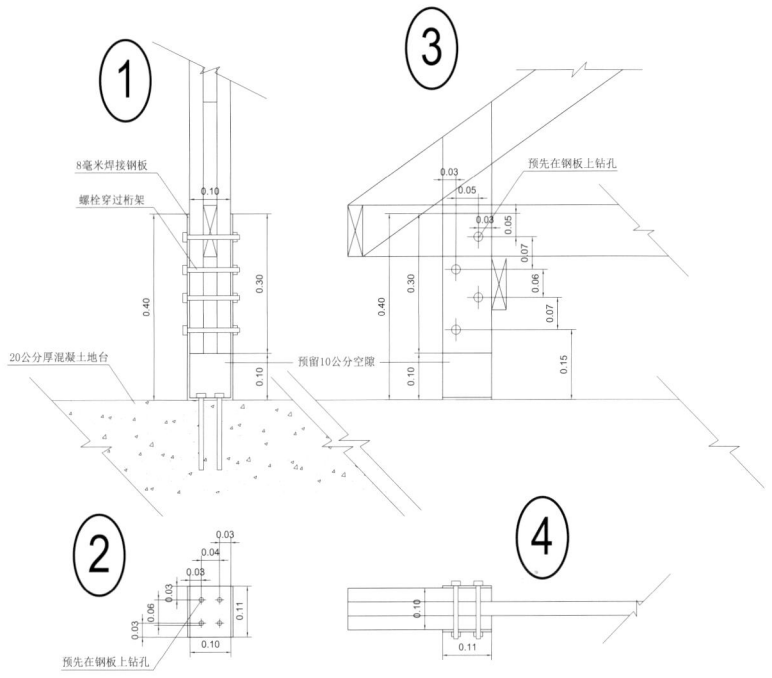

1. Draw centerline on ring foundation;

2. Shift four main footings from central axis 46.5 cm clockwise;

3. Subdivide spaces between the four main footings into three equal parts;

4. Double check that spacing between each footing is approx. 1.42 meters;

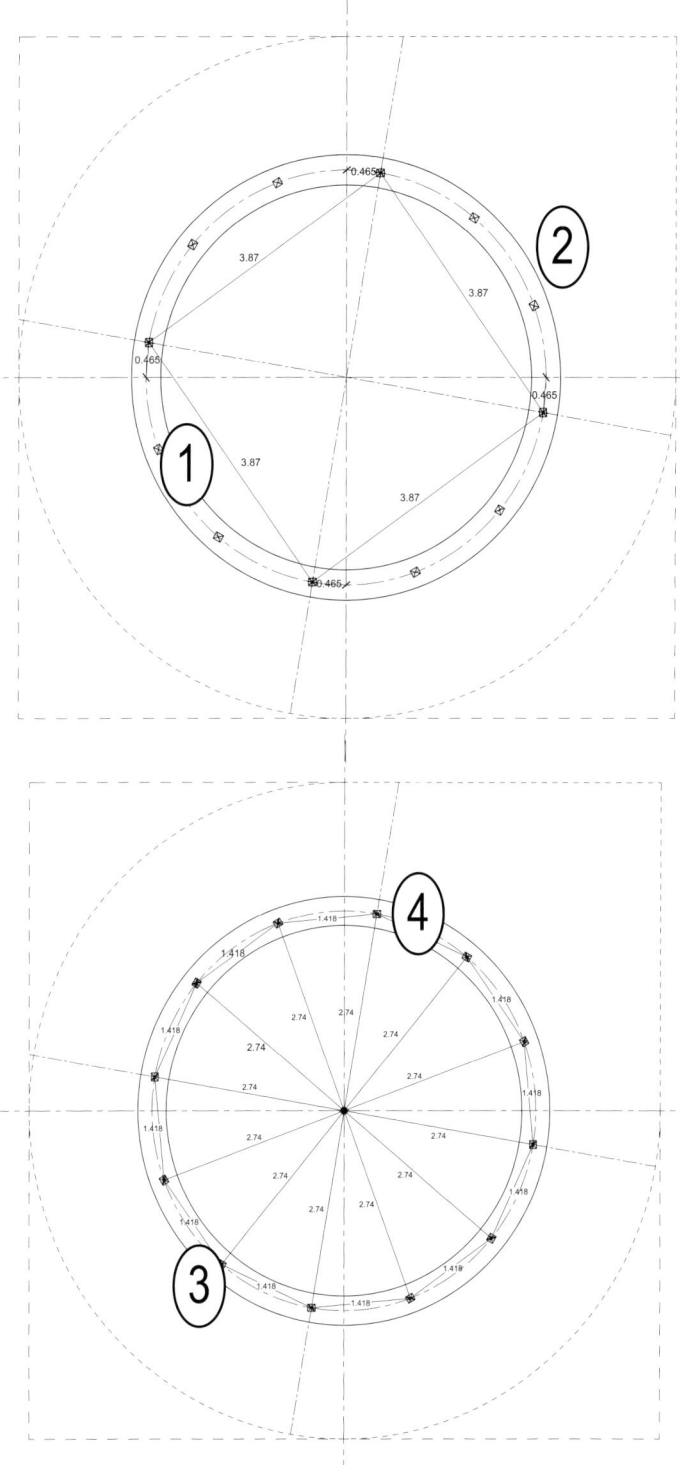

1   Catalog of 12 trusses descending from high

2   to low,

3   and raising to high again;

4   Principal outer lines are single layer whereas inside lines are double layered;

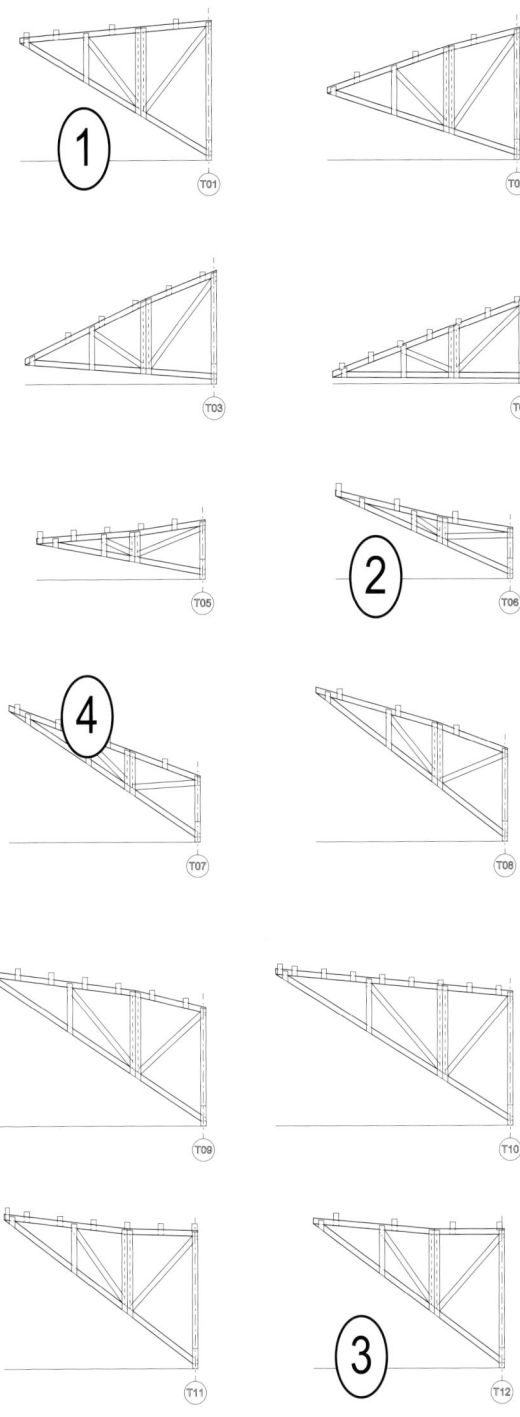

1. All trusses are made of a sandwich of three layers, to be fabricated flat adjacent to construction site (same as Pinch);

2. Main lines are single inner layer;

3. Secondary lines are double outer layers;

4. Attach beams stoppers onto top element of truss at specified locations—see reference T01;

T02 平面图
T02 plan

T02 横梁定位板尺寸及位置
T02 beams stoppers

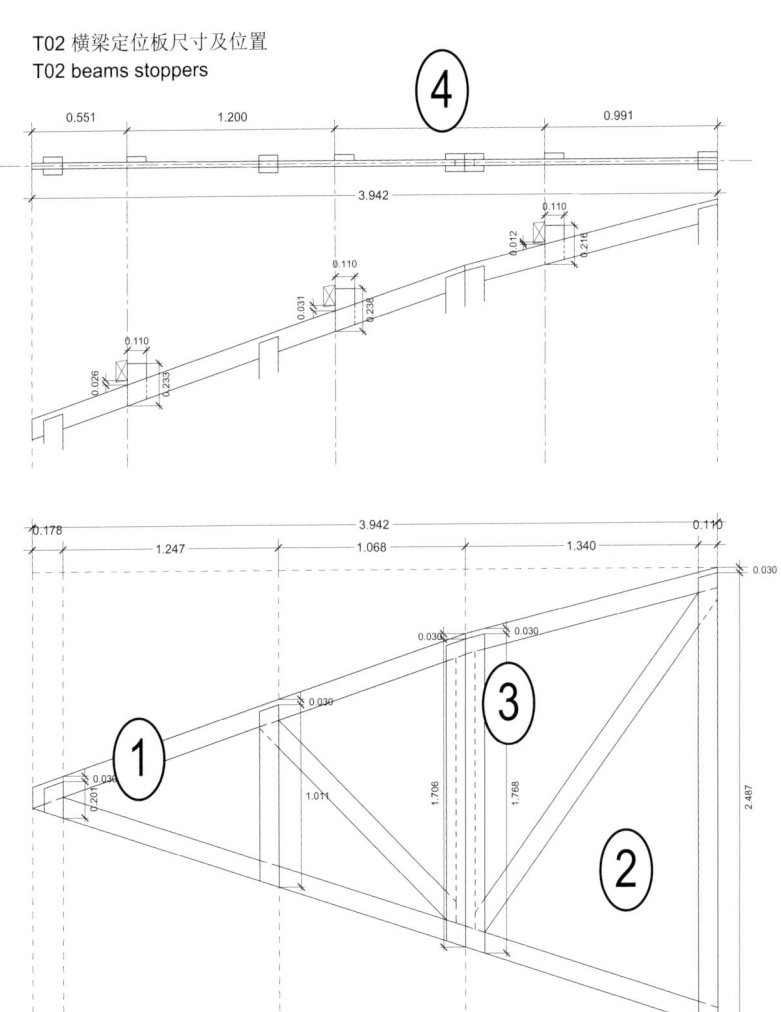

T02 木桁架外层（双面）　　比例1：20
T02 outer layer (double)　　scale 1:20

Site cleaning with local villagers.

Scaled model is used as a tool for communication between students and local builders.

Live construction with architecture students and a team of local carpenters.

EXAMPLE 9: WARP

1   The ground is sloped—need to build a stepped foundation with retaining wall;

2   Align columns longitudinally in three rows to account for the main trusses;

3   Straight ruled beams to be placed perpendicular to the trusses;

4 Decking to run in the same direction as main beams;

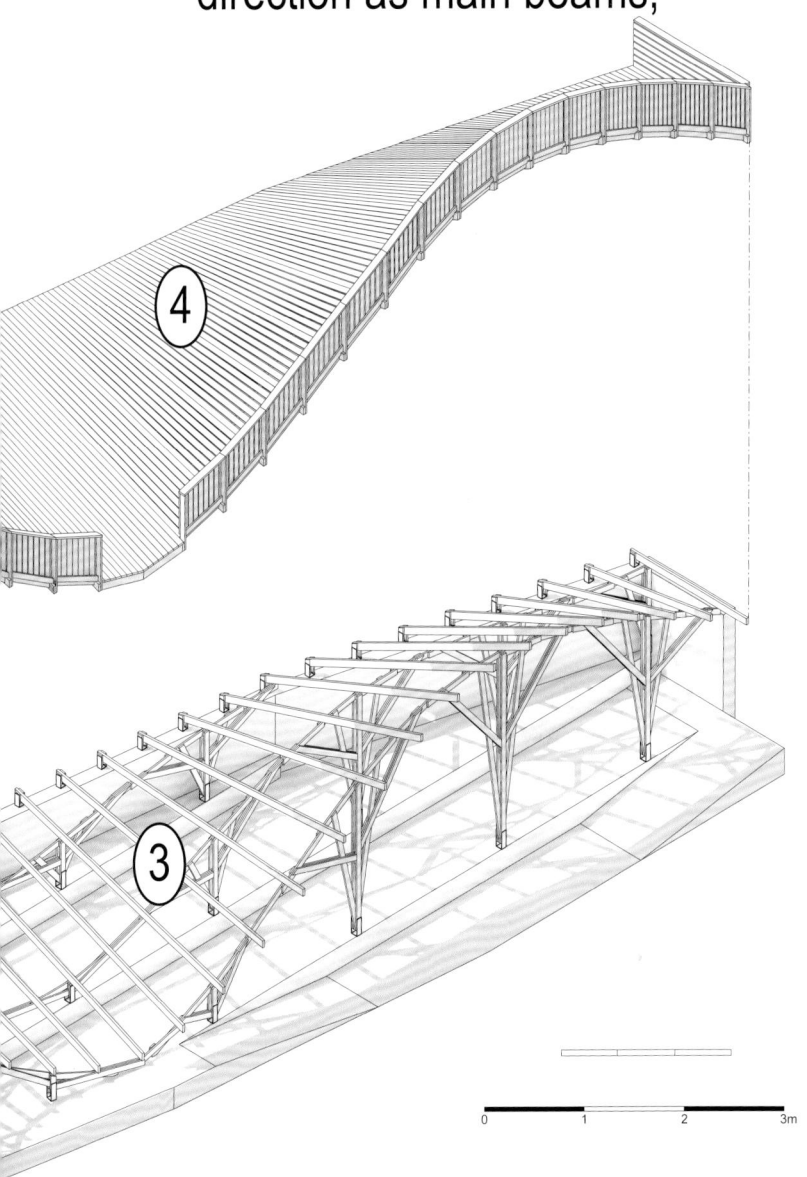

AXONOMETRIC VIEW

1   That's how the front elevation will look like: From sine curve to straight line with resting space below;

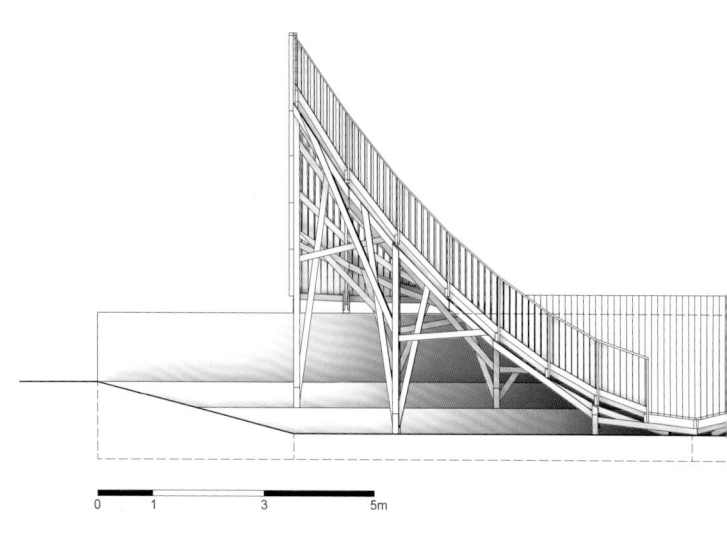

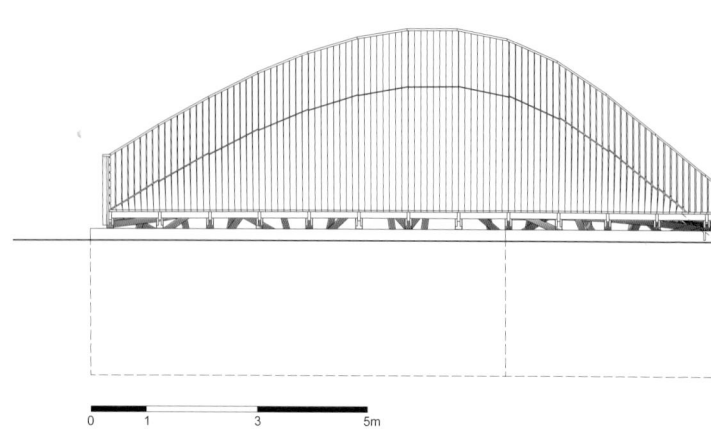

232

2. In the back elevation the roof goes from straight line to sine curve—you can rest on top of the roof;

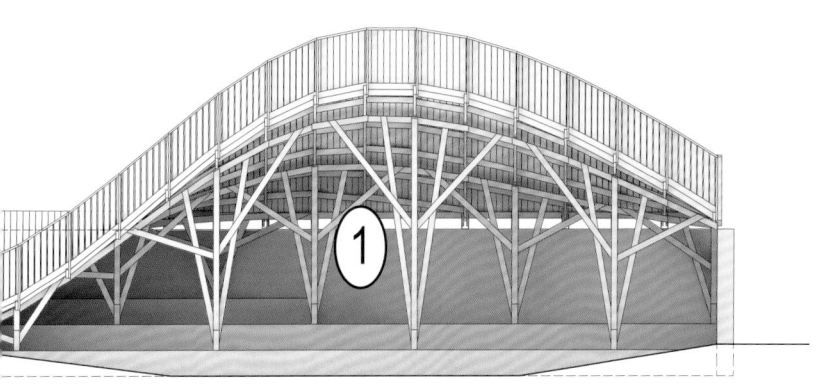

BACK ELEVATION

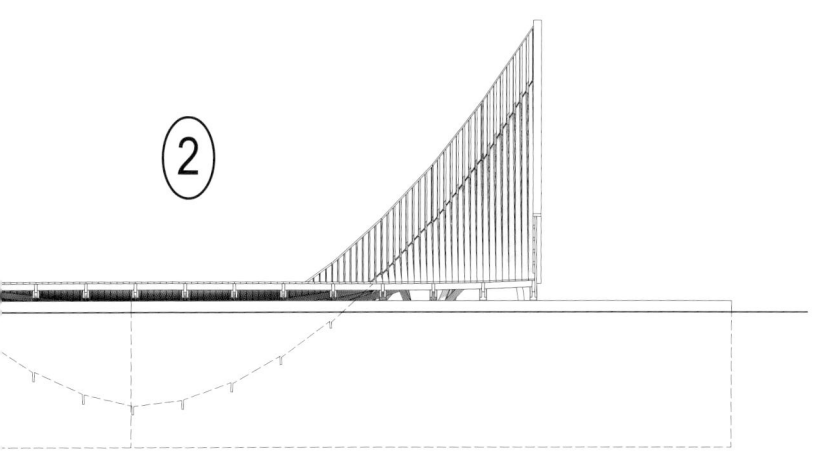

FRONT ELEVATION

1. Important! Always refer to the (0,0) for all measurements (see plan drawing);

2. The finishing of the retaining wall MUST be levelled and smooth!

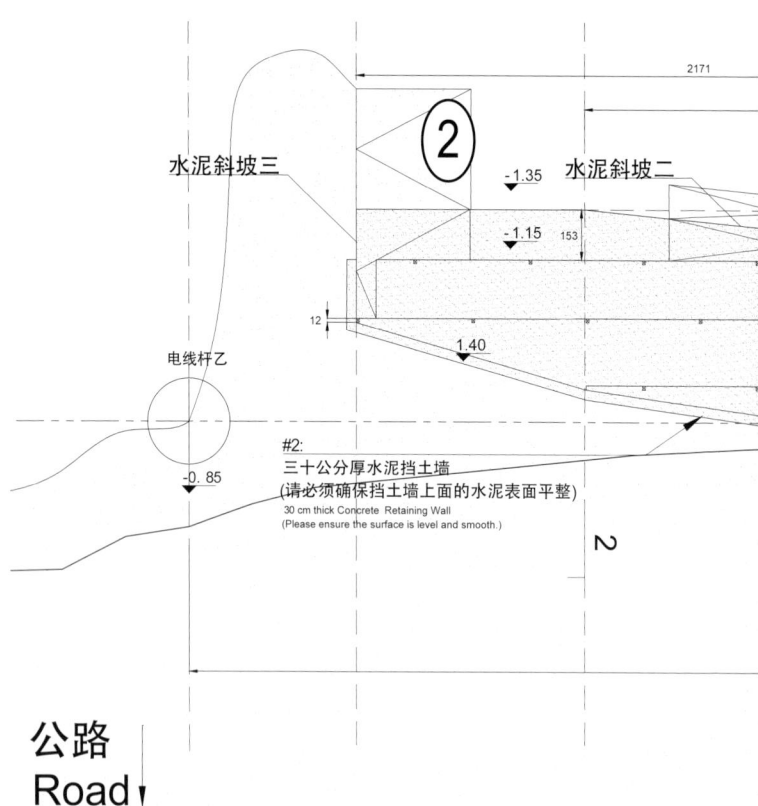

3 Please communicate with contractor: wooden columns to be installed on the edge of the steps. Again: edge of concrete surface must be levelled!

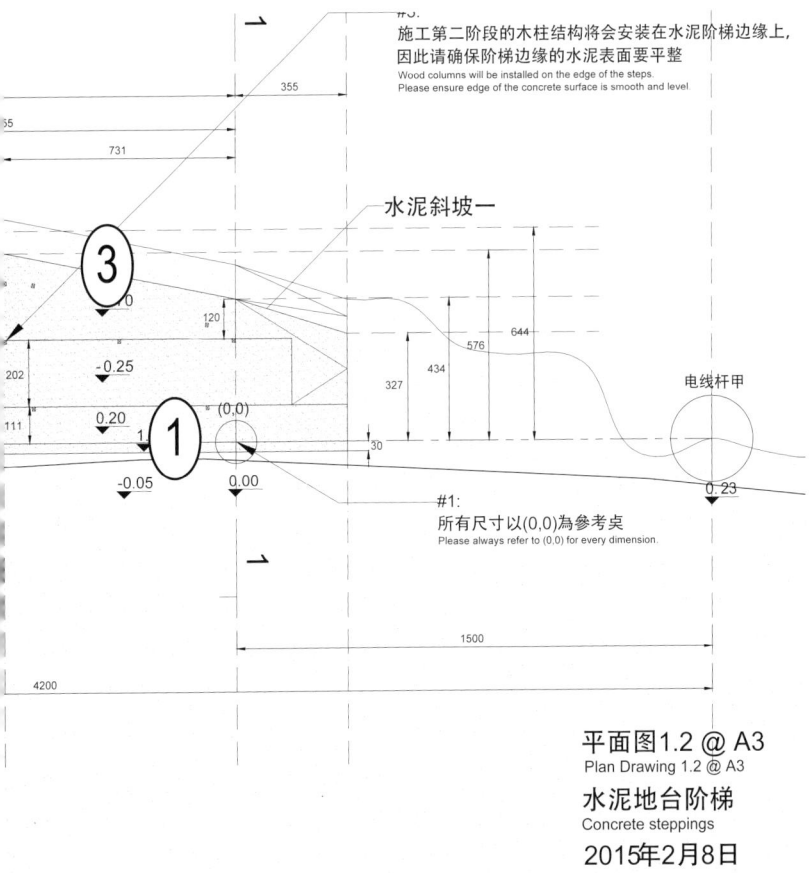

Plan Drawing 1.2 @ A3
Concrete steppings
2015年2月8日

1 Contractor needs to have this ASAP—first thing to do is to excavate accordingly and build the four retaining walls;

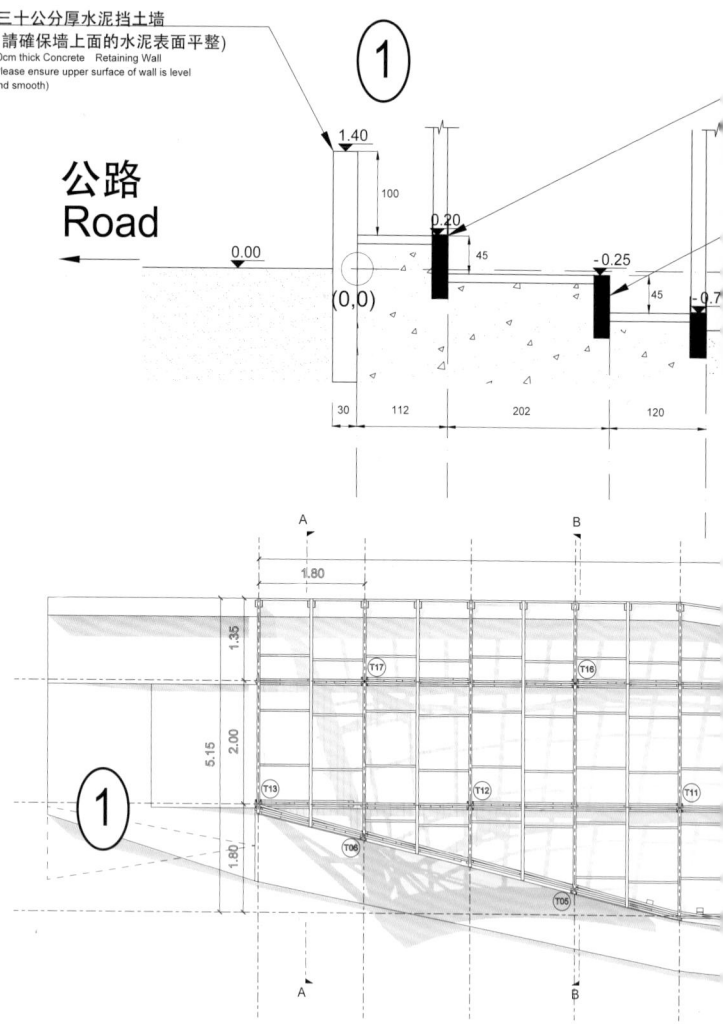

三十公分厚水泥挡土墙
(請確保墙上面的水泥表面平整)
30cm thick Concrete Retaining Wall
(Please ensure upper surface of wall is level and smooth)

公路
Road

施工第二阶段的木柱结构将会安装在水泥基墙上面，
因此请确保阶梯边缘的水泥表面要平整
Wood columns will be installed on the edge of the steps.
Please ensure edge of the concrete surface is smooth and level.

二十公分厚水泥基墙
20cm thick Concrete Foundation Wall

-0.90

山谷
Valley

剖面图1-1 @ A3
Plan Drawing 1-1 @ A3

水泥阶梯基墙结构
Concrete steppings foundation walls

2015年2月8日

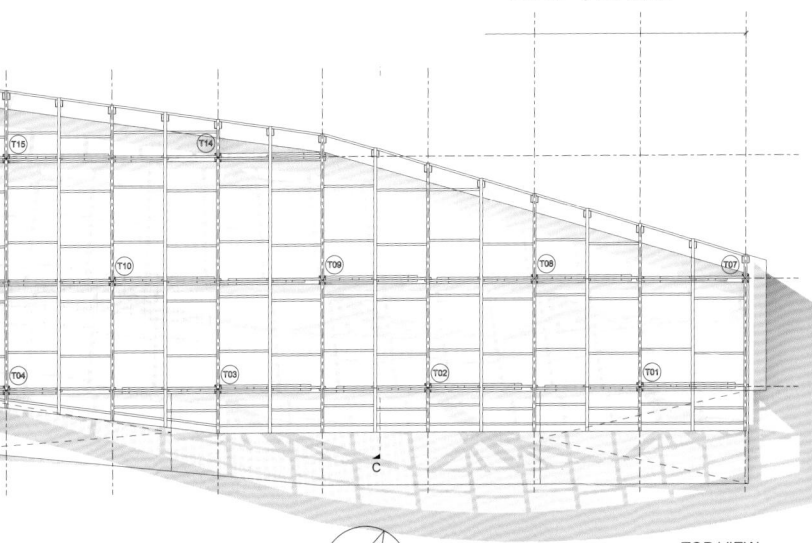

TOP VIEW

1   Catalog of fanning columns for the three main structural bays;

2   Each column is to be prefabricated flat and bolted in a sandwich of three layers (same as Pinch and Sweep);

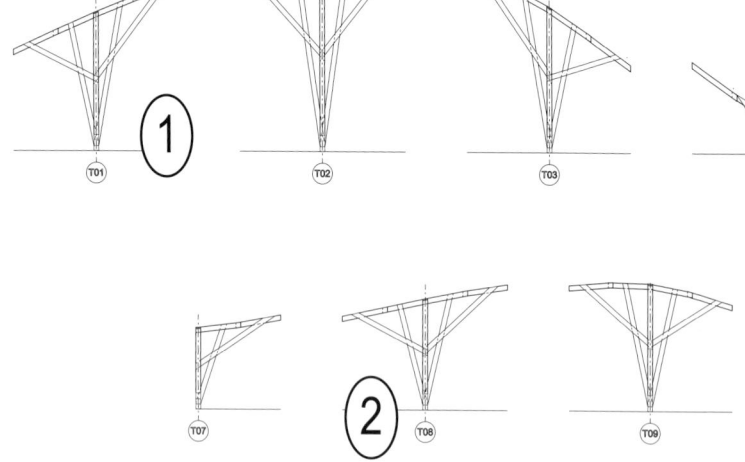

3   Central column of trusses = doubled and outer layers;

4   Diagonals and top edge of trusses = single and inner layer;

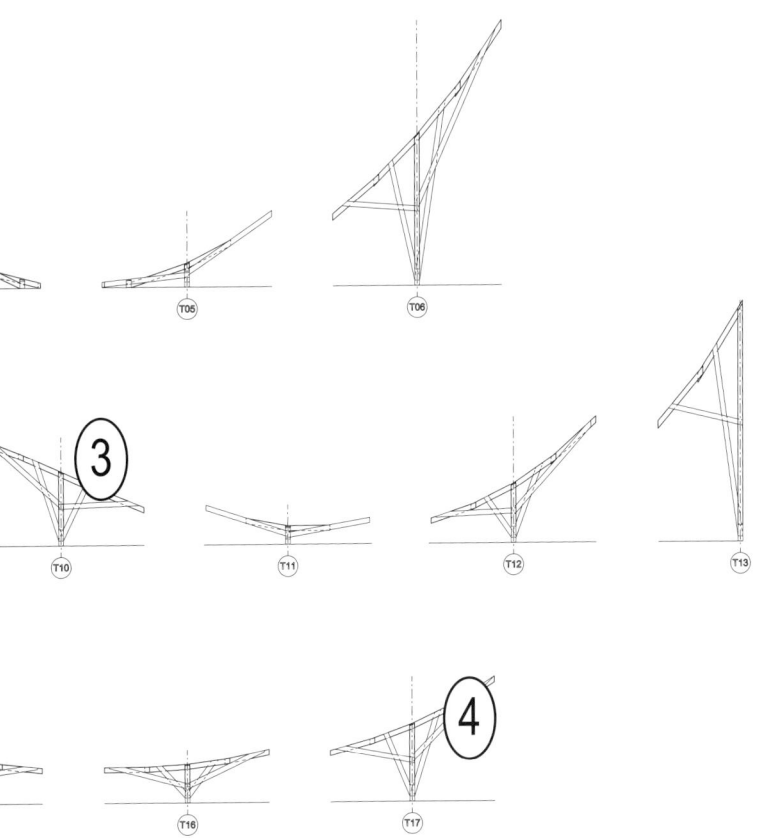

Our construction drawings are redrawn by local carpenters one-to-one on the pavement to guide the prefabrication of the trusses.

In-situ construction of the retaining walls and foundation by local villagers.

Placement of straight beams on top of timber trusses to receive final decking.

Teams of architecture students collaborate with local builders in the construction of the timber structure.

An on site decision was to integrate concrete steps with the main retaining wall to accommodate the need of local street vendors.

RESPONSIVE FORMWORKS
Interview by Rainer Hehl (RH)
with John Lin (JL)
and Olivier Ottevaere (OO)

(RH) John and Olivier, I'd like to begin with the title of your book, *Uncertainty*. If we look at the finished outcome of the last project in the book, Wavelength, we might not be aware of how far uncertainty played a significant role during the design and construction process. To a large extent, the materialization of the building was driven by the invention of a construction procedure rather than a predefined formal expression. When did you encounter moments of uncertainty?

(OO) One of the biggest moments of uncertainty was in the transition between experimenting with construction techniques in our lab at the University of Hong Kong, to the making of prototypes and finally having to jump to an architectural scale. In a much larger sized project, you have to respond to different kinds of material forces. I think that was the first moment. The question of how we were going to engage in that scaling-up and if the builders would be able to take it into their own hands and translate the work into a full-scale architecture.

(RH) You developed the project in Hong Kong, but then suddenly confronted it with the local

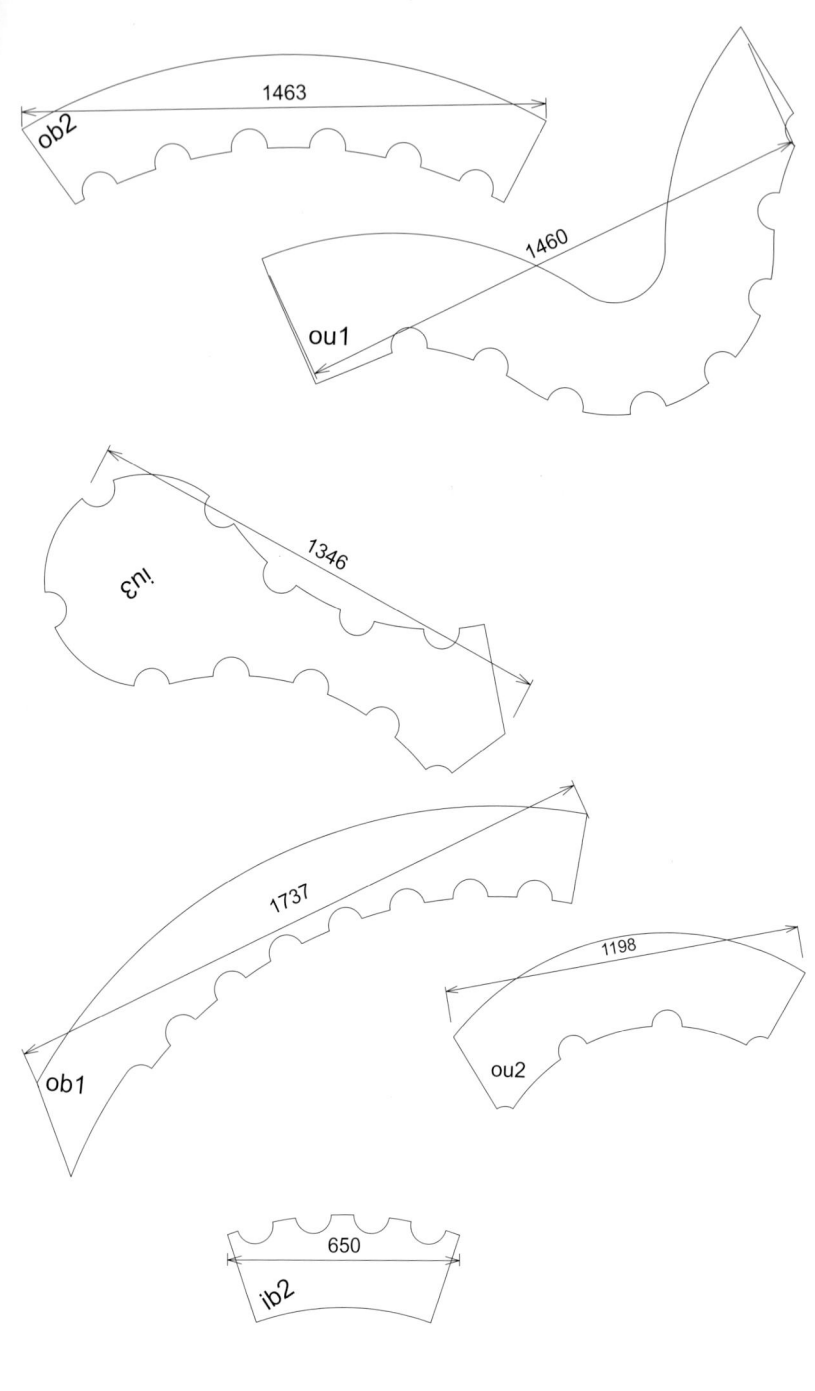

conditions on site. So it was the construction site itself, which became some sort of laboratory for a culture of making; and as a matter of fact, you designed a construction process that was never tested before and you had to enter unknown territories. Experimentation on tectonics turned out to be a very specific way of knowledge production and transfer, which relies on an intense dialogue between design and building practice. How did you manage to establish this close relationship with local actors? How did you convince people to undergo this experiment and what was the framework allowing this experiment with uncertain outcome to happen?

> (OO) It was a lot of back and forth, involving a lot of site visits to explain and show how things could be done. Suddenly, the contractor felt this urge to try it himself through a series of mockups on site. The first one was a disaster, a complete failure. Then, progressively, by calibrating the material, choosing the right size of the bamboo poles, and testing types of fabric they finally got to a result that was promising enough to test in an architecture scale. It was still a risk but we shared a kind of faith that it would turn out. But honestly, we didn't know until the concrete was poured and set. Only at that moment we knew it worked.
>
> There is a key vehicle, which facilitated the construction process: that's geometry. We were quite aware of the limitations of available skills and materials. What was guiding the formwork was their linear geometry. We had to rationalize the double-curved shell with straight lines, which became

Left: Plywood templates as part of the formwork for the location of bamboo poles.

bamboo poles. The gaps left in between were taken care of by the fabric. These register the force of concrete; liquid pressure that is imprinted on the bottom surface of the grid shells.

(RH) It seems that the geometry defined the outline of the project and at the same time it acted as a mediator between the design intention and technological possibilities. The geometric figure of the drawing established the basis for the dialogue but also allowed you to embrace a certain degree of uncertainty regarding the final outcome.

> (JL) I think there are also other conditions that allowed for the uncertainty to occur. If you look at the way that projects are made in China, politically, financially, even socially, there is a space of ambiguity. In China, the client usually approves a rendering—an image of the project. This can be both limiting and liberating. I know many architects find themselves constrained by this. But the space it opens up is the freedom to develop the technical and logistical considerations after the project is approved. We were working with principal ideas rather than an exact set of drawings. I think this space allowed us to work with the builders in an experimental way to make this project feasible.
>
>> (OO) A lot of the design decisions were made on the construction site together. On our visits with the government and the contractor, we were making a lot of changes, adjusting things, addressing other things in different ways; which in Europe or the US would be

Right: Full-scale prototype of bamboo and fabric formwork ready for concreting.

impossible, because it typically costs a lot of money to make any changes. Whereas in our experience, it was actually welcome that we were constantly there—we had an ongoing discussion with them, trying to see how we can solve certain aspects that were not completely resolved.

(JL)   Its quite interesting, because we could follow the development of the construction and consider our solutions one step at a time. For instance, as the project proceeds hierarchically from foundation to structure, facade then infill; each decision could be taken based upon the execution of the former. It was a practice of leaving space for resolution and the acceptance that many decisions can't be fully anticipated.

(RH)   By leaving space for things to happen, for ideas to develop, you were able to react as you moved forward with the project, while also getting in direct connection with contextual conditions. You established some kind of on-site-activism, which allowed for a very intense confrontation with the local context.

(JL)   Exactly. I think that it allows for an even more site-specific work. I think we can acknowledge there is so much you can't completely anticipate just from making models and drawings. Take for example, Louis Kahn during the construction of the National Assembly Building in Bangladesh. He observed how the workers used formwork for casting the concrete walls that would leave gaps every five feet. By filling

Left: The responsive formwork comprised of inner and outer layers of fabric and bamboo poles with steel reinforcement in between.

in these gaps with inlaid white marble, they give the monolithic concrete walls a sense of scale and become its primary expression. Another example of Louis Kahn's willingness to make radical changes to the design based on his experiences while on site is the design of the roof over the main assembly hall. He continued to alter and change the design for the roof until almost the entire structure and walls were built. I think this demonstrates how much you can't imagine beforehand, until the actual construction. That's the mystery, I think, of making architecture.

(RH)   You are talking about how uncertainty is important if you look at projects in the history of architecture. But it seems like nowadays the building industries are pretty much standardized and relate to very controlled ways of operation. So, the very interactive way of dealing with the design process seems pretty much related to the specific situation of rural China and also its specific economy. Can you talk about the framework of the economy within which you were operating and how that might still be different from the conventional mode of construction processes in the "west"?

> (OO)   More and more, buildings are assembled or their assemblies are modular. There is a reliance on manufacturing and prefabrication; so, a lot of things are built off-site, brought to site, and then put together. It is very difficult to deviate from this process, making it impossible to evolve design live with construction. The unique aspect of the context we're working in is that buildings are still completely built in-situ. The processes may be perceived as linear, but it actually opens up a lot of

opportunity because it is made on the spot, and we can respond to how things are made on the spot. Going on site and learning how those tradespeople and craftspeople are working, their technique really influences how we made some of our design decisions. So, a lot of the gaps and as a result the invention were filled in by the workers in terms of their own imagination and their expertise in knowing what can be done.

(JL)   There is a lot about this project which could not have been built in the west. For all its sophistication and building knowledge, the ways things are built in the west are based upon guaranteeing economic certainty. We were also initially pushed to build this with lightweight steel—it would have been far easier to calculate structurally and cost wise.

(OO)   It is another form of tolerance.

(RH)   It might be important to read the project in the context of the revival of traditional architecture in the Chinese countryside, and how the government is trying to promote these technologies in order to address questions of identity. You could say it is a trend in using the skills of local labor. But in your own particular case, the project was not necessarily based on traditional technologies but rather on inventing a certain way of vernacular building practice. Can you talk about your specific approach within the context of this revival of traditional models and building types in rural China?

(OO)   The way we were responding to identity, locality, and tradition was through the palette of materials we've been using. We can reuse them in a more counter-imaginative way. So, I think that gives it its own presence and it fits into that context but then on the other hand, the space and tectonics created are completely different.

(JL)   Our approach to the question of tradition and how to express it is to see our project as a link between the past and the future, not just a revival of the past. I think one of our ambitions is allowing the project to be as specific as possible—specific to the conditions of the site, its climate, materials, and its culture of making.

(RH)   So instead of just looking for an iconography of vernacular building types, your approach is on developing something that might not refer to the image of traditional architecture but emerges from using the local resources and skills, establishing something that is pushing the limits of what is possible with traditional technologies. Do you think that this experiment is unique, and how far could this lead to a very specific development of building culture in rural China? To what extent do you see your project as something that can innovate building practice and be adopted by these local practices and how far do you think that this experiment is kind of closed?

(OO)   I don't think it's closed.

(JL)   I do think that it's possible to influence the local building culture. First of all, it's very cheap and made with generic materials. So, we've done something that looks quite different, but within the same budget,

Right: The formwork is easily peeled off once the concrete is cured.

so they can easily emulate it. We are also relying on their expertise with bamboo—but by giving them a different manifestation or expression for this material, we're expanding upon these techniques.

(RH)   It is interesting to see that you were confronted with basically two types of construction modes. One which is highly controlled, which is about efficiency, and the determination of the project through very precise drawings. And on the other hand, we have building practices which is about testing, which is about adaptation. It is a very empiric way to conceive architecture, which by definition also relates to vernacular architecture. In your case, you combine and control to an extent and you also relate to informal vernacular practices. Do you think there is still space for this within the context of rural China; isn't it also becoming more and more controlled? Where are there still opportunities for introducing very professionalized knowledge into local, informal, or popular building processes?

>   (OO)   The gap is definitely closing in China. It is getting harder and harder, but I think it's still possible in contexts and cultures where there's no preconceived idea of how something should be built. We've found that the willingness to experiment is culturally and politically embedded but it's not like this all across China. It is getting more and more regulated, more and more regimental. There are many more kinds of protocols, rules, building codes, especially in the city and urban areas.

(JL)   Our interest in working with the vernacular allows us to consider what this means as a design process, not just a stylistic issue. The traditional craftsperson works in a reactionary way; there is no exact model of a house, but relational principles and a set of constructional elements that can be adapted directly to the site. We're trying to learn from it and connect it to our own experience with industrial materials and constraints. I think we're trying to discover moments of co-existence between two very different methods of design; beyond the aesthetic considerations.

I think our approach is not about what it looks like, but how we build it, and allowing that process to arrive at a natural outcome. It may seem simple, but we learned it from the craftspeople. Their power is that they don't have a fixed product in mind, but are able to resolve problems in incremental fashion. You could say they have a toolbox or language that they work from.

Even though modern architecture is fixated on the idea of flexibility and "openness," it is generally from a spatial or programmatic understanding. It is still formally driven. And so of course embracing other forms of "uncertainty," requires a level of risk taking. And this contravenes the nature of contemporary architecture practice, which is all about mitigating risk.

(RH) There is one aspect I am curious about if we think about uncertainty in the context of China. Even though you are projecting a strong narrative, you're also facing a lot of contradictions: between tradition and modernity, between handicrafts or hand-skill and high technology, but also between being anchored in local tradition and also being part of a global culture. So how far do you see that these contradictions are offering possibilities and do you believe that rather than looking for ideal conditions, contradictions can actually trigger new ways of conceiving and producing architecture.

> (JL) I think you're absolutely right in the sense that what is possible is generated because of the way we are working. But it may also reflect the current situation in China, which is simultaneously very high-tech and low-tech. The contradictions you bring up result from the rapid urbanization process, and I believe there is still much unrealized potential. We continue to discover new possibilities and linkages, but it is definitely a space of freedom.
>
>> (OO) It's a challenge to design without any preconceived images or references. But that's necessary in order to take advantage of local conditions (or even contradictions).

(RH) For me, what is particular and innovative in your project is your focus on tectonics. Innovation is usually connected to guiding themes or keywords that might be relevant for today's transformations, whether it's sustainability or social change, and translating these themes into architecture. But in your case, you are actually going into the basics of construction: into core questions of how to assemble materials together and how to make it possible in terms of skills and labor. It seems to me that the innovative potential lies in the process of going back to the roots.

EXAMPLE 10: WAVELENGTH

1   The roof should recall the surrounding landscape of peaks and valleys—concrete for the down parts (1) and timber for the peaks (2);

2   The timber roof connects to the concrete shells but MUST appear seamless—how do we detail it?

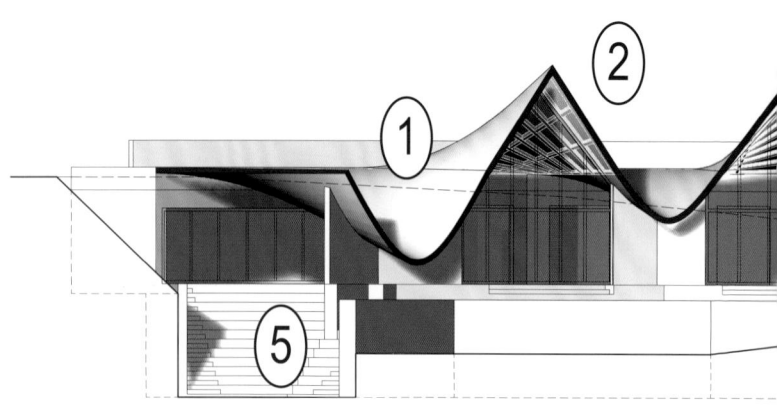

3   Please refer to detail drawings for depths and widths of concrete shells—they are all different!

4   Here is where the access from road behind should be—to double check with site plan;

5   The view from here should be wonderful! Stairs to below terrace should be big enough to serve as viewing sitting area, not only circulation;

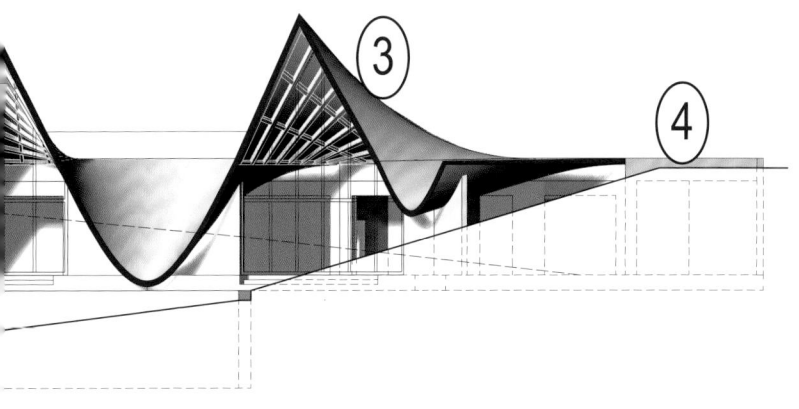

1   About the interior space,
    I think placing the ramp from
    parking level here is the best
    option.

2   From the ramp you get to the
    open reception right
    below one of the
    concrete
    shells.

3   Here I was a thinking about a bar area with panoramic terrace. What do you think?

4   Imagine here the outdoor terrace levelled with the open reception …

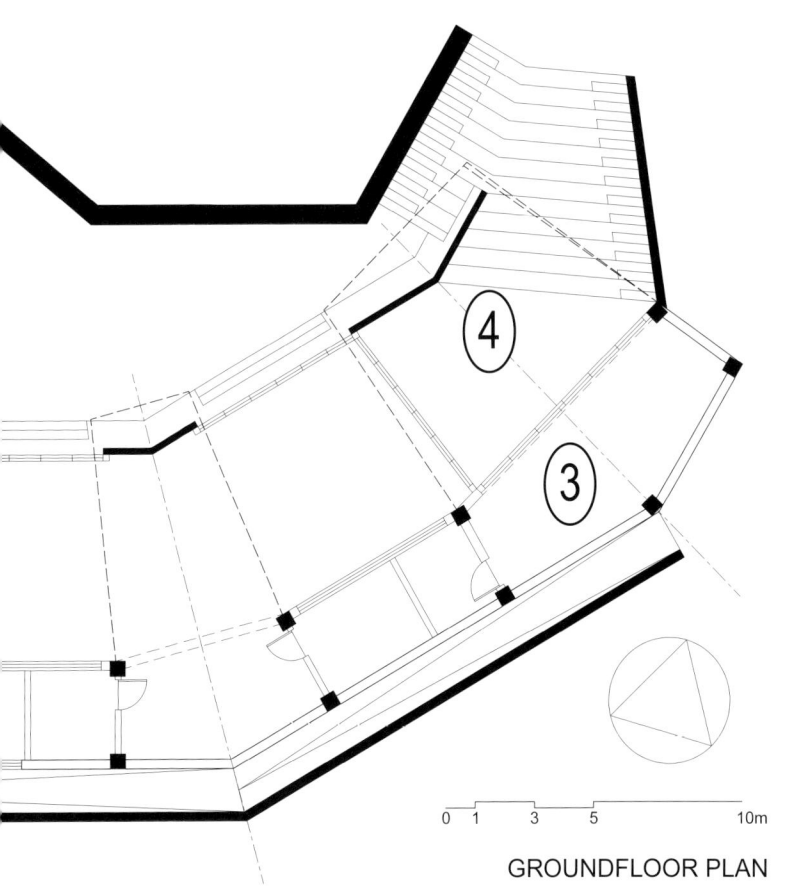

GROUNDFLOOR PLAN

1   Make sure the contractor gets it right—scaffolding + bamboo poles + canvas, and then concrete to be cast onto one-way responsive formwork;

2   Obviously, between the bamboo poles there will be gaps and that's where the construction canvas comes into play;

3   Bamboo poles describe the linear geometry of the doubly curved shell;

4   Timber templates will register all the curved two-dimensional profiles onto which the bamboo poles rest;

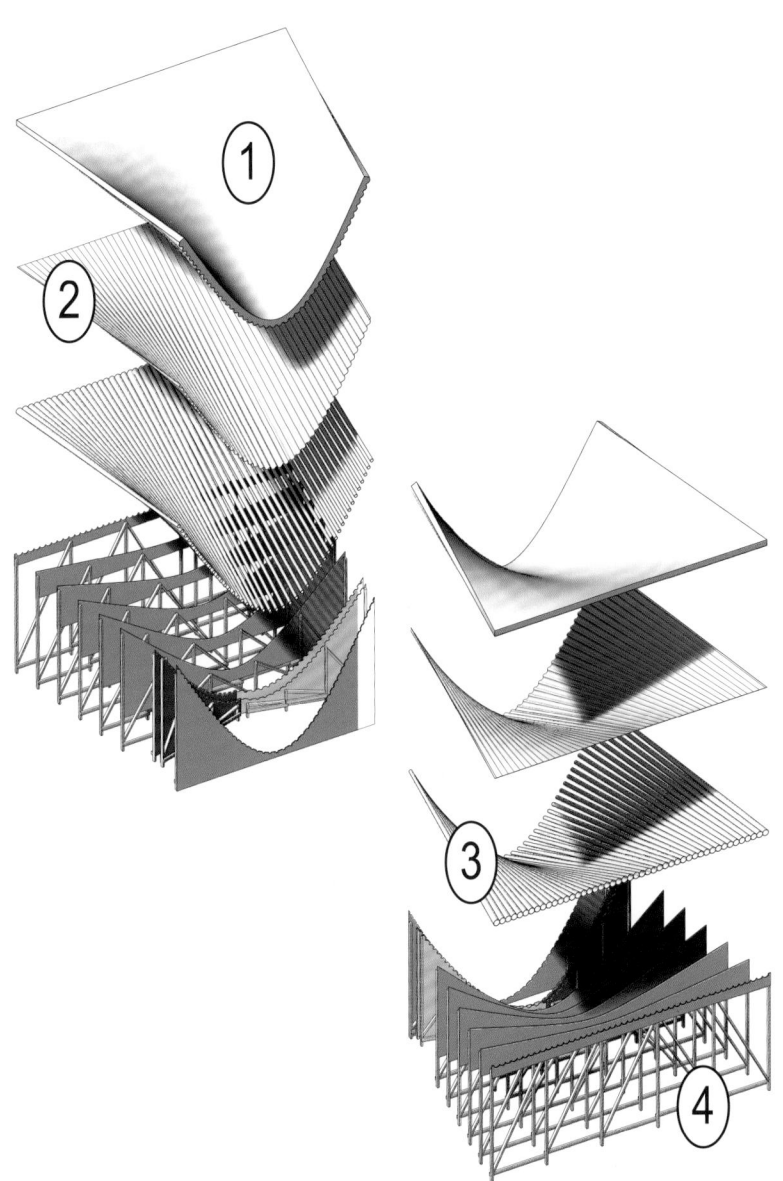

1   Here you have the concrete shells as a series of two-dimensional bays from flat (A9) to the most curved section (A1)—always double check measurements and refer to drawings!

2   The curved plywood profile is held by the steel scaffolding. The position is very specific and must be verified;

3   Bamboo poles to be positioned and fastened straight onto the curved plywood;

4   The canvas is stapled onto the length of each bamboo pole (I recommend to try the process on a small 1:1 prototype first);

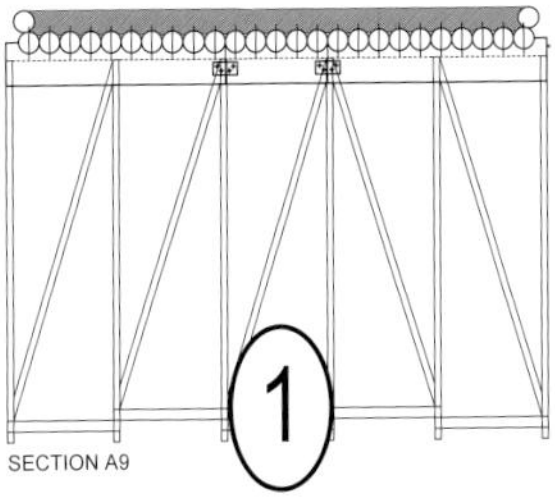

SECTION A9

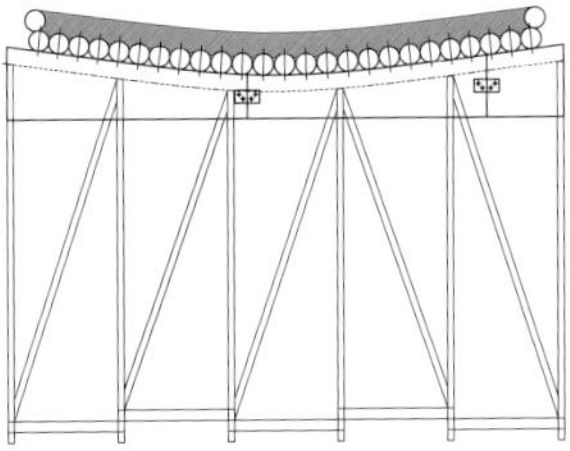

SECTION A8

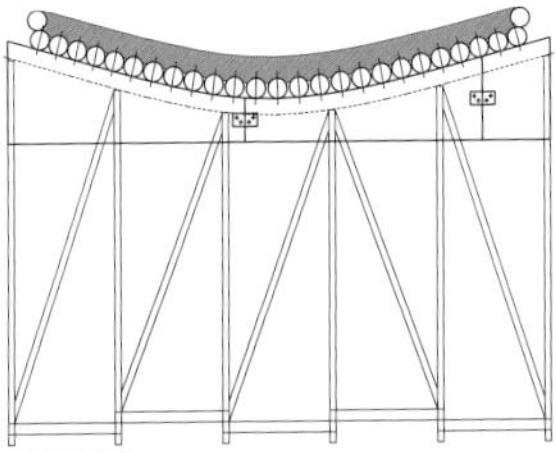

SECTION A7

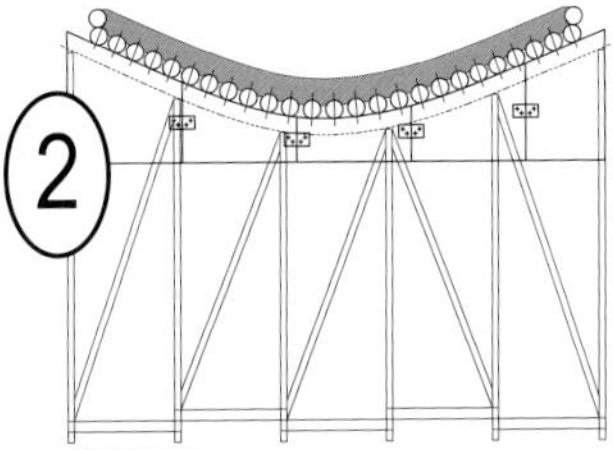

SECTION A6

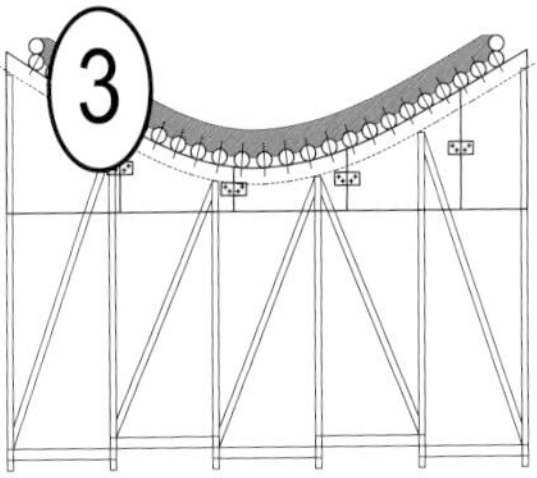

SECTION A5

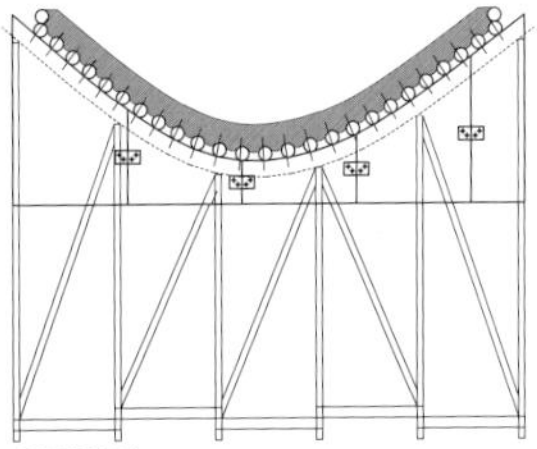

SECTION A4

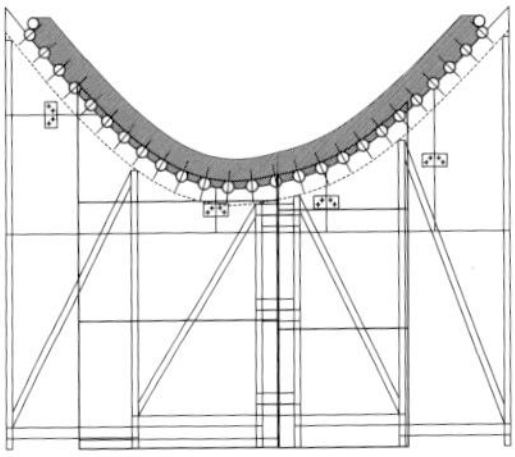

SECTION A3

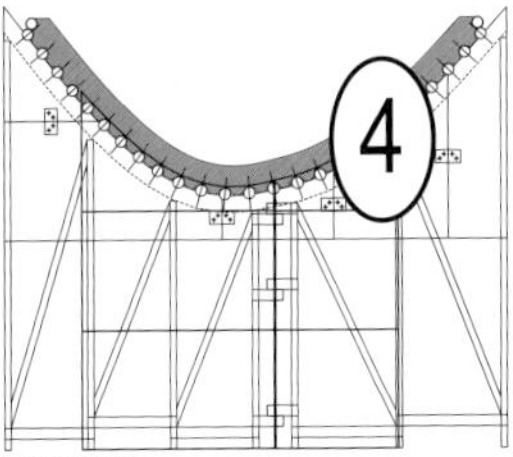

SECTION A2

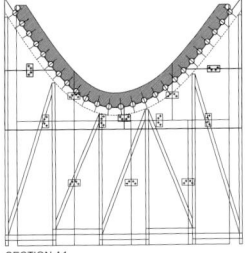

SECTION A1

1. As explained already—here you have all the bays of the shell in plan (A1-A9)—refer to sections if needed. The edge plywood profile is fundamental to control the thickness and proper finish of concrete!

2. Gap in the formwork to simultaneously cast the wall support below the shell: monolithic construction!

3. Bamboo poles to be first placed tight against each other;

4. Progressively gaps open up between each for the fabric to interact with the liquid concrete;

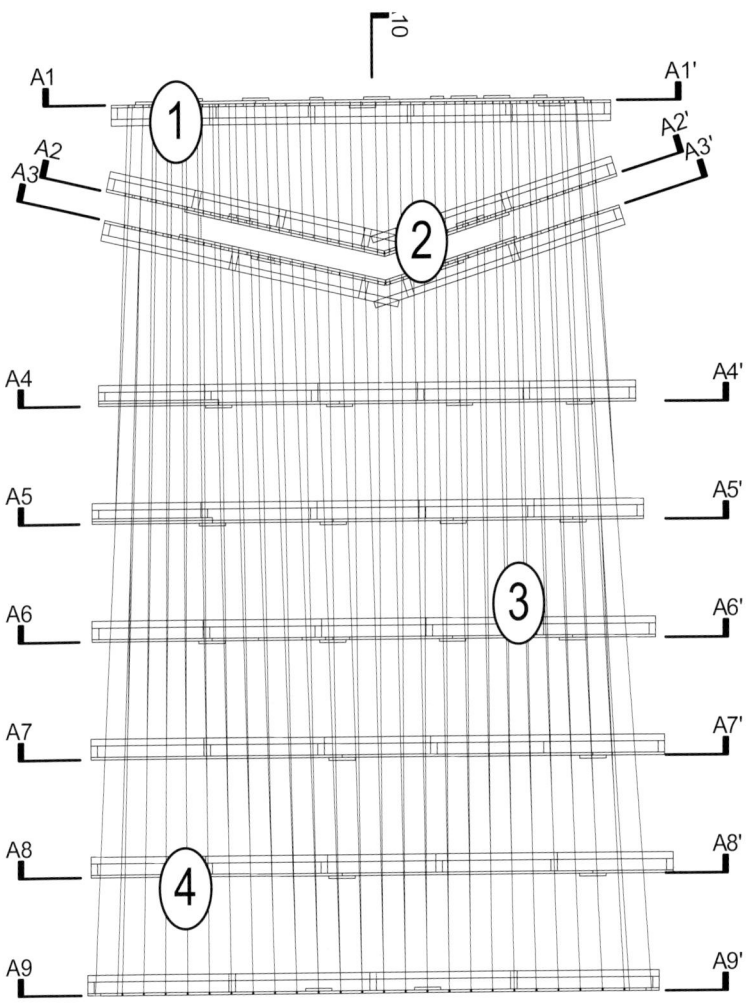

With no road access, inventive means had to be implemented to carry the construction materials down the slope.

The contractor had to pursue a series of full-scale mock-ups to ensure he could master the formwork technique.

View of Wavelength during the concreting of the four shells, making up its main structure.

Carpenters levelling the curved templates of the formwork to guarantee the proper locations of the straight bamboo poles.

Workers securing the bamboo poles onto the shells' scaffolds.

Gaps open between poles as they are progressively run down the sloped formwork.

Sheets of fabric are then stapled directly onto the poles to cover the gaps and complete the formwork.

One of the formworks of the main shell being completed prior to concreting.

Under belly of one of the shells after removing the formwork showing the corrugated impression of the bamboo poles and fabric onto the surface of the concrete.

Concrete formwork being removed while the timber roofs are being constructed.

Resting on the concrete shells, the main trusses of the timber roofs span from a flat to a high-pitched profile.

PART 2
CERTAINTY

CREST

CREST

LANTERN

LANTERN

WINDOW-STAIR

WINDOW-STAIR

STAIR-TOWER

STAIR-TOWER

STAIR-TOWER

WIND AND RAIN BRIDGE

WIND AND RAIN BRIDGE

SUN ROOM

SUN ROOM

SUN ROOM

PINCH

PINCH

SWEEP

SWEEP

WARP

WARP

WARP

WARP

WAVELENGTH

WAVELENGTH

WAVELENGTH

PROJECTS CREDITS

1) CREST
Project Leader: Olivier Ottevaere, Department of Architecture, the University of Hong Kong
Design Team: Chad McKee, Yvonne Meng (project manager), Weijen Wang, Department of Architecture, the University of Hong Kong
Student Participants: He Yizhen, Ji Xiang, Liu Kaixuan, Sun Kexuan, Song Huiqing, Romeo Chang, Kevin Lai, Chan Shuman, the University of Hong Kong, Department of Architecture
Contractor: Anji ZhuJing bamboo technology co. LTD.
Client: Lingfeng management committee of Anji County, Zhejiang Province.
Location: Anji, Zheijang, China
Completion Year: 2017
Size: 150sqm
Construction Cost: 70,000 RMB

2) LANTERN
Project Leaders: Donn Holohan, Olivier Ottevaere, Department of Architecture, the University of Hong Kong
Design Team: Ruby Huang (project manager)
Student Participants: Leung Lok Yan, Jiang Xinjie, Pu Chunpeng, Ng Hei Ting, Wang Yadian, Hui Tsz Nam, Tang Xiao, Tan Regina Tania, Cheung Wing Lam
Contractor: Anji ZhuJing bamboo technology co. LTD.
Client: Lingfeng management committee of Anji County, Zhejiang Province.
Location: Anji, Zheijang, China
Completion Year: 2019
Size: 80sqm
Construction Cost: 220,000 RMB

3) WINDOW-STAIR
Project Leader: John Lin, Department of Architecture, the University of Hong Kong
Design Team: Chiara Oggioni, Lau Bo Yee, Yi Sun
Student Participants: HKU and HKDI Architecture Students 2019
Funding: the Hong Kong Jockey Club Charities Trust, Shizhong County Government
Contractor: Liu Landscape Engineering Ltd.
Client: Shizhong County Government
Location: Lantian Village, Longyan, Fujian Province
Completion year: 2019
Size: 20sqm
Construction Cost: 195,000 RMB

4) STAIR-TOWER
Project Leader: John Lin, Department of Architecture, the University of Hong Kong
Design Team: Lau Bo Yee, Chiara Oggioni, Yi Sun
Student Participants: HKU and HKDI Architecture Students 2019
Funding: the Hong Kong Jockey Club Charities Trust, Shizhong County Government
Contractor: Liu Landscape Engineering Ltd.
Client: Shizhong County Government
Location: Lantian Village, Longyan, Fujian Province
Completion year: 2019
Size: 20sqm
Construction Cost: 195,000 RMB

5) WIND AND RAIN BRIDGE
Project Leader: Donn Holohan, Department of Architecture, the University of Hong Kong
Design Team: Elspeth Lee, Jiang Hejia (team leader) HKU Architecture Students 2016
Funding: Supported by the Gallant Ho Experiential Learning Fund, HKU
Contractor: Peitian Community Craftsmen
Client: Peitian Village Government
Location: Peitian Village, Fujian Province, China
Completion Year: 2016
Size: 20sqm
Construction Cost: 120,000 RMB

6) SUN ROOM
Project Leader: Donn Holohan, Department of Architecture, the University of Hong Kong
Design Team: Elspeth Lee, Jiang Hejia (team leader) HKU Architecture Students 2017
Funding: Supported by the Gallant Ho Experiential Learning Fund, HKU
Contractor: Peitian Community Craftsmen
Client: Peitian Village Government
Location: Peitian Village, Fujian Province, China
Completion Year: 2017
Size: 20sqm
Construction Cost: 70,000 RMB

7) PINCH
Project Leaders: John Lin, Olivier Ottevaere, Department of Architecture, the University of Hong Kong
Design Team: Crystal Kwan (project manager), Ashley Hinchcliffe, Connie Cheng, Johnny Cullinan, Jacky Huang, Joyce Ip, Yvonne Xu Meng
Funding: Supported by the Knowledge Exchange Impact Award, HKU
Contractor: Kunming Dianmuju Shangmao Company
Client: Shuanghe Village Government
Location: Shuanghe Village, Yunnan Province, China
Completion year: 2014
Size: 80sqm
Construction Cost: 130,000 RMB

8) SWEEP
Project Leaders: John Lin, Olivier Ottevaere, Department of Architecture, the University of Hong Kong
Design Team: Crystal Kwan (project manager), Connie Cheng, Gabriel Chan
Student Participants: Year 1 class, HKU Architecture Students 2014
Funding: Supported by the Gallant Ho Experiential Learning Center, HKU
Contractor: Kunming Dianmuju Shangmao Company Ltd.
Client: Tuanjie Village Government
Completion year: 2014
Location: Tuanjie Village, Yunnan Province, China
Size: 60sqm
Construction Cost: 90,000 RMB

9) WARP
Project Leaders: John Lin, Olivier Ottevaere, Department of Architecture, The University of Hong Kong
Design Team: Joyce Ip (project manager), Jason Chong, Tod Zhu, Yvonne Xu Meng
Student Participants: Year 1 class, HKU Architecture Students 2015

Contractor: Kunming Dianmuju Shangmao Company Ltd.
Client: Ludian Village Government
Funding: Supported by the Gallant Ho Experiential Learning Fund and a Knowledge Exchange Grant, HKU
Completion year: 2015
Location: Ludian Village, Yunnan Province, China
Size: 130sqm
Construction Cost: 180,000 RMB

10) WAVELENGTH
Project Leaders: John Lin, Olivier Ottevaere, Department of Architecture, The University of Hong Kong
Local Architect: Xingcun (Ben Zhang and Guan Huilong)
Design Team: Josephine Saabye, Zubin Singh, Xia Chengwei, Liu Chang, Bo Yee Lau, Haotian Zhang, Chiara Oggioni
Client: Baojing Local Government
Contractor: Baojing First Construction Company & Hunan Zhipeng Construction Company
Location: Baojing, Hunan Province, China
Completion year: 2021
Size: 2570sqm
Construction Cost: 14 million RMB

IMAGES COPYRIGHTS
P176 & P179: Félix Candela Book Original Images; Félix Candela Papers, C1455, Manuscripts Division, Department of Special Collections, Princeton University Library.

BIOGRAPHIES

John Lin is an architect based in Hong Kong and an associate professor at the University of Hong Kong. He is a director of Rural Urban Framework (RUF), a research and design platform dedicated to developing sustainable prototypes for rapidly urbanizing areas. The approach combines research into large scale processes of urbanization with the integration of local construction practices and contemporary technology into built projects. His recently published book *As Found Houses* (AR+D Publishing, 2021) documents the unexpectedly innovative ways that rural self-builders adapt, modify, graft, cleave, and wrap their traditional homes. It is the research context for his current teaching and design projects: experimenting with ways of living which is neither rural nor urban, but both traditional and modern.

Olivier Ottevaere is an architect and educator based in Hong Kong. He is the founder of Double(O) Studio and an associate professor in practice at the University of Hong Kong. His interest in architecture is driven by a hybrid approach between physical experiments and geometrical organizations. Integration of active structural principles, live properties of materials, and inventive procedures of construction prompt the design pursuit at the onset of each of his projects. Trefoil House in Lisbon, Portugal, as part of his broader practice-research work on prototyping with concrete, puts forward a built architecture where material, structure, mass, scale, and space has become one entity inseparable from the user's experience.

Donn Holohan is an architect based in Hong Kong and Ireland. He is an assistant professor at the University of Hong Kong and a founding partner of multidisciplinary design studio Superposition. A trained cabinet maker, his research centers on building culture and the climates, tools, and materials that shape it. Through the integration of emerging technology with local and vernacular knowledge, his built work seeks new modes of construction and tectonic expression that are both informed by and responsive to the places and people they serve.

Something Fantastic was founded by Elena Schütz, Julian Schubert, and Leonard Streich based on the conviction that architecture is related to everything and the resulting social, ecological, and political responsibility demands a different practice. The work of the "undisciplinary" office includes research and teaching in addition to the conception of books, exhibitions, furniture, buildings, and urban planning. Having tought the MAS Urban Design at ETH Zurich, for several years the partners have now heading the Space Department at the Gerrit Rietveld Academie in Amsterdam; their current visiting professorship at the Peter Behrens School of Architecture Düsseldorf is entitled "All-inclusive Urbanism."

Rainer Hehl is an architect/urban designer and is currently guest professor for construction and architecture design at the TU Berlin where he is also dean of Studies of the international Masters program (M-Arch T) with a focus on typology. In addition to having lectured widely on urban informality, popular architecture, and hybrid urbanities, Rainer Hehl holds a PhD from the ETH Zürich on urbanization strategies for informal settlements focusing on case studies in Rio de Janeiro.